MARCO POLO

RHODES

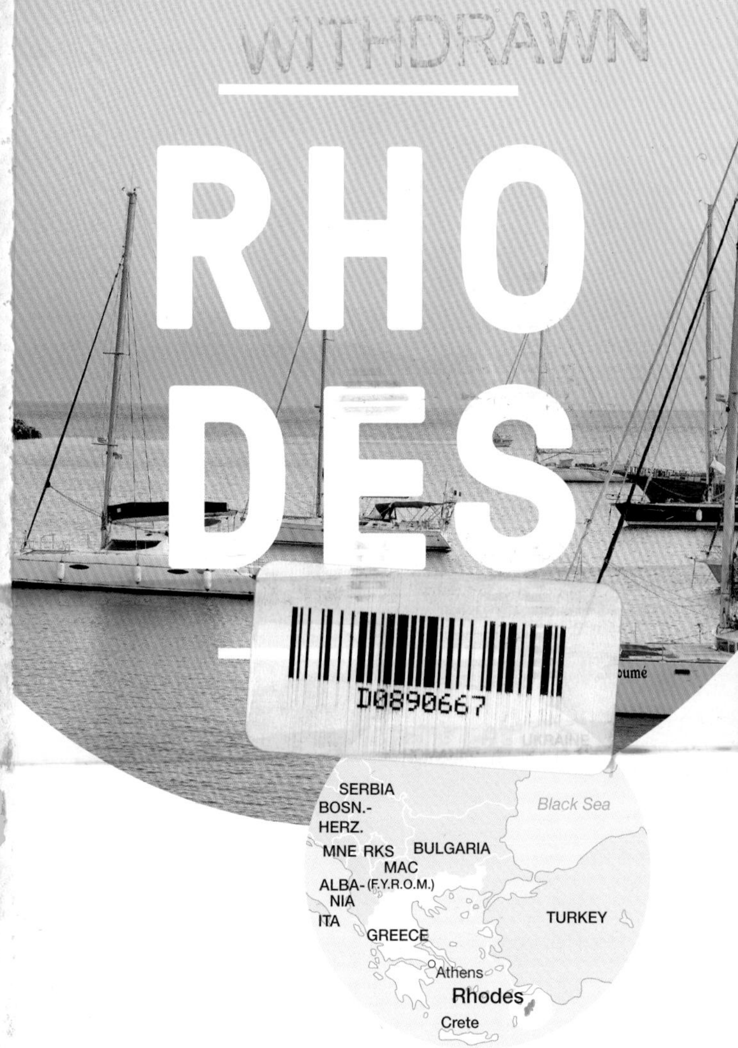

www.marco-polo.com

FREE!
THE
TOURING APP
shows you the way...
including routes and offline maps!

GET MORE OUT OF YOUR MARCO POLO GUIDE

IT'S AS SIMPLE AS THIS

1 go.marco-polo.com/rho

2 download and discover

GO!

WORKS OFFLINE!

SYMBOLS

 Insider Tip
★ Highlight
●●●● Best of...
Scenic view
Responsible travel: fair trade principles and the environment respected
(*) Telephone numbers that are not toll-free

PRICE CATEGORIES HOTELS

Expensive	over 140 euros
Moderate	70–120 euros
Budget	under 70 euros

Prices per night for two persons in double room without breakfast in peak season

PRICE CATEGORIES RESTAURANTS

Expensive	over 20 euros
Moderate	12–20 euros
Budget	under 12 euros

Prices for a meal with main course, accompaniment and salad, without drinks

 On the Cover: Faliráki's rocky coves p. 77 | Rhodes' Old Town p. 34

DID YOU KNOW?

Timeline → p. 14
Local specialities → p. 28
Luxury in the face of crisis → p. 40
For bookworms and film buffs→ p. 60
National holidays → p. 105
Currency converter → p. 109
Budgeting → p. 110
Weather → p. 111

MAPS IN THE GUIDEBOOK

(118 A1) Page numbers and coordinates refer to the road atlas
(0) Site/address located off the map
(U A1) Coordinates refer to the map of Rhodes Town inside the back cover

(⊞ A–B 2–3) refers to the removable pull-out map

INSIDE FRONT COVER:
The best Highlights

INSIDE BACK COVER:
Map of Rhodes Town

The best MARCO POLO Insider Tips

Our top 15 Insider Tips

INSIDER TIP **Beach alternatives**

The crowds flock to the main beach at Faliráki. But just a stone's throw away, there are *four small rocky bays*, easy to reach on foot from the big hotels. Just follow the coastal road north! → **p. 77**

INSIDER TIP **Romantic (k)nights with air conditioning**

At the *Cava d'Oro* in Rhodes Old Town you stay in a 700-year-old house – the only hotel with a private staircase up to the city wall → **p. 46**

INSIDER TIP **A day at the ranch**

Relaxing close to nature at the *Elpida Ranch:* lots of greenery, an improvised pool, nice people, horses for hacks, a small archery facility and cuddly animals → **p. 98**

INSIDER TIP **A dip at the ends of the Earth**

Strangers hardly ever venture out to the two *pebble beaches at Cape Foúrni* below Monólithos (photo right) → **p. 54**

INSIDER TIP **Eating "Germans"**

In the taverna *En Plo* in Stegná, the rare brown rabbitfish is served. The Greeks call this fish *Germanos,* so they find it amusing to watch as German tourists eat this fish → **p. 76**

INSIDER TIP **In veggie heaven**

In the mountain village of Laérma, the *Ingo* taverna serves up grilled vegetables on large platters. They also contain *pitaroúdes* – probably the island's best veggie patties → **p. 66**

INSIDER TIP **Day trip to Sími**

Oooh and Aaah: When the ship enters the harbour of the neighbouring island of *Sími,* everyone takes a picture. The main town is an idyll like it may have been 200 years ago (photo left) → **p. 48**

INSIDER TIP **Timeless jewellery**

Time stands still at *Níkos Vassiláras* in the Old Town. He makes pendants from old clockworks and each piece is a unique item → **p. 44**

INSIDER TIP A mountain village holiday

If you stay at *Hotel Thomás* in Monólithos, you will find yourself among locals. Sign up for cooking classes, take part in extensive wine tastings or rent a mountain bike a no extra cost → **p. 53**

INSIDER TIP Classy souvenir

In Kiotári you can bring along your washed-up treasures from the beach and have them *set in silver* – a very special and unique souvenir → **p. 65**

INSIDER TIP Made in Greece

Is there such a thing as Greek fashion designers? You'll find the answer at *Blue Eye* in Líndos. Or alternatively in the Old Town of Rhodes at *Haris Cotton* → **p. 60, 43**

INSIDER TIP First dive

If you're new to scuba diving, the *Vasilía* will take you to Rhodes' *dive sites* for a first taste of an oxygen mask in the undersea world 5–6 m (approx. 16 ft) below the surface → **p. 97**

INSIDER TIP Young Greek nights

Many Rhodians leave the discos in Faliráki in the hands of the tourists. They prefer to meet in the music clubs around the *Ibrahim Pascha Mosque* in the Old Town → **p. 45**

INSIDER TIP Everything within reach

Verandas directly on the seafront. A small harbour with rustic tavernas just two minutes on foot. The island's raving nightlife just around the corner? Sound appealing? Then the *Aquarius* Hotel in Faliráki is made for you → **p. 78**

INSIDER TIP Sweet society

Housed in a former officers' casino, the *Aktaíon* is the island's most venerable establishment when it comes to the best ice cream, cakes and gateaux. A more upper class society meet up here, both day and night → **p. 41**

BEST OF...

GREAT PLACES FOR FREE

Discover new places and save money

FOR FREE

● ***Tour of the ramparts***

A stroll through the park-like *ramparts* in Rhodes Town will give you an idea of the colossal task facing the Ottoman invaders who lay siege to Rhodes in the 16th century. In contrast to the city walls, access is free and possible at all times → p. 39

● ***Cycling through the forests***

If you stay at the Hotel *Élafos* on the mountain Profítis Ilias or just stop by, you can rent one of the mountain bikes standing next to the front door at the reception desk for free and head off into the thick forests of the island's second-highest mountain → p. 83

● ***A lap of the modern stadium***

On Monte Smith you'll find the remains of an ancient temple, a theatre and a *stadium,* accessible day and night. Feel free to do a few laps on the running track, no one will stop you – and there's no admission charge or entry fee! → p. 38

● ***Picture book of faith***

The church in the *Thári* Monastery near Láerma is decorated entirely with frescos. They tell stories from the Bible, which you can look at without paying for the privilege. With a bit of luck, you might even be invited for a mocha by the monks (photo) → p. 66

● ***Conquering castles***

The strenuous long walk up to the medieval castles of *Archángelos* and Charáki on the east coast and *Kritinía* and Monólithos on the west is definitely worth it – the entrance is free of charge → p. 73, 81

● ***Great perspectives – in every respect***

From the *Tsambíka* Monastery, high up above the east coast, you can enjoy one of the finest Rhodes panoramas. Taking a free look at the guest book of the Virgin Mary will also give you a perspective on the motives of those locals who have made the pilgrimage up here → p. 83

ONLY ON RHODES
Unique experiences

● *Dancing under the stars*
Rhodians prefer to spend balmy summer evenings outdoors so the open-air discos are quite popular. One of the largest is the *Ampitheatre Club* near Líndos where guests dance under the stars with a magnificent view of the bay and the castle bathed in moonlight → p. 61

● *Picnic with a view*
At the chapel *Ágios Geórgios Kálamos* high above the Aegean Sea, you can sit in the shade under the trees at the tables for the parish fair and enjoy a picnic with a view across the sea to the neighbouring islands → p. 51

● *A visit to the synagogue*
Rounding off the multicultural mosaic that is Rhodes, the *synagogue* in Rhodes Town is worth a visit. Representatives of the small community, which was re-formed after the Holocaust, give you an insight into their history and faith → p. 40

● *Saturday night among Greeks*
Rhodians party from midnight into the early hours of Sunday morning in the tiny *Café Chantant* situated in the Old Town of Rhodes. Whiskey bottles on the table, ten-piece orchestra on stage and traditional Rembétiko music played for the crowds of dancers → p. 45

● *A classic coffeehouse*
At the *Café Aktaeíon* in the capital, judges and lawyers get together In the mornings while the elegant ladies of Rhodian society gather here in the afternoons. There's also a constant stream of people with time on their hands, both young and old → p. 41

● *Rustic village*
The mountain village of *Mesanagrós* paints a fine picture of the decline of the island villages in the pre-tourism days of the 20th century → p. 54

● *Feasting at Mama Sofia's*
Things that Rhodians love to eat and which tourists hardly ever find on their plates are on the menu here in this taverna in Rhodes Town. Scary-looking *foúskes,* for example (barnacles) or *simiaká* – shrimps, which are even tinier than the ones you know from home → p. 42

BEST OF...

AND IF IT RAINS?

Activities to brighten your day

● *Sheltered refuge*

A pleasant place to sit, sheltered from possible wind and rain, is the inner courtyard of the fine market hall *Néa Agorá* in Rhodes Town → p. 38

● *Heavenly hour*

The interior of the *Evangelismós Church* at Mandráki harbour in the island's capital is completely covered in large frescos in the traditional Byzantine style – a perfect opportunity to test your knowledge of the Bible → p. 40

● *A glass of wine*

At the winery of the *Triantáfillou* family, winemaker Jáson invites you to talk shop at an extensive wine tasting. When it stops raining, he will take you on a tour of the vines – on request even on the back of a horse → p. 72

● *A knight's castle steeped in history*

The *Palace of the Grand Masters* in Rhodes Town is an ideal place to while away the time on rainy days. Exciting exhibitions give an insight into the day-to-day life in the days of the knights and of antiquity (photo) → p. 35

RAIN

● *Permanently wet*

Creatures that never feel the rain on their skin can be seen close up at the Art Déco *aquarium* on the northernmost tip of the island. You will also stumble upon some curious animals such as a one-eyed ape and a calf with seven hoofs → p. 100

● *Head for shelter*

A tourist cannot leave Rhodes without buying an umbrella first. No other island in the Aegean has a larger selection of umbrellas than Rhodes. When it starts to rain, head for the stores around the *Platía Kyprou* in the New Town → p. 43

RELAX AND CHILL OUT

Take it easy and spoil yourself

● ***Wellness in the captain's house***

The wellness and beauty centre *Spa Líndos* with its modern furnishings is located in a stylish 100-year-old captain's house in Líndos. Treat yourself to a day of pampering and let yourself unwind at this day spa → **p. 61**

● ***Stop in any time***

You can spend an entire day at *Koúkos* in the new part of Rhodes Town. Enjoy breakfast on the sunny terrace across from a church and eat lunch on one of the cosy balconies on the first floor. In the afternoon, coffee and cake are served with coffeehouse flair while candlelit tables await dinner guests before live music streams from the pub – all under one roof → **p. 41**

● ***Skip across the water***

You don't need a boating licence in Stegná to rent a *motorboat* and leisurely explore the bays of the area at your own tempo. Rent one at the beach and set off after a quite quick driving lesson → **p. 97**

● ***An evening at the casino***

Spend a relaxed evening at the elegant *casino* in Rhodes Town. The flair of a James Bond film mixes with an oriental feel inside (photo) → **p. 45**

● ***Greek cuisine on the roof***

At the *Archontiko* in an old captain's house in heritage-protected Líndos you can savour fine Greek cooking on the roof terrace with its romantic view over the white-painted village towards the Acropolis and the sea → **p. 59**

● ***Fishing at Mandráki***

Fishing is for many Rhodians the height of relaxation. Those who don't have their own boat sit on the jetty, rod in hand, gazing out towards Asia or the Old Town and waiting for "the big one" to bite. There is no need for a fishing licence → **p. 37**

INTRODUCTION

DISCOVER RHODES!

Your descent by plane starts when you reach the Aegean. From the sky out of the windows on the left, the Turkish coastline and Greek islands almost blend into one with the boundary between ***Asia and Europe*** melting together. Rhodes then appears out of the sea: the island is not a flat atoll but abounds in forests, mountains and beaches. You are about to land in paradise: Parádisi is the name of the village where the airport is also located.
Days full of discoveries and emotions await you. Rhodes is Greece's fourth largest island, almost half the size of Mallorca. Take a closer look at the map before your visit. To the south of the island lies Prassoníssi, a long stretch of sandy beach covering the tip of the island and a mecca for windsurfers from around the world. To the north is Rhodes Town, home to the largest intact and ***most beautiful old town in the Aegean***. The straight-line distance between both is 70 km/43 miles.

If you want to plunge straight into Greek life, your first port of call should be the island's capital. The best and cheapest way to travel there is by bus. Depending on your bus driver's age and taste, you will be accompanied on your journey by sounds of Greek rock or

Photo: Líndos Bay

traditional folk music. The bus is sure to be decorated with family photos on the windscreen as well as an icon of a saint to protect passengers on their journey.

At the end terminal you have the choice between the ancient and modern, between the city and the sea: on the one side the ramparts and towering ***fortifications of the Old Town***, on the other shops and boutiques sell the latest fashion labels and umbrellas. There are ***cafés*** everywhere, most of which attract a fashionable crowd. Before a shopping trip, take a seat here, slow down, soak in the sights and sounds around you. The waiter will often bring a bottle of water for you to quench your immediate thirst. Water is a sign of hospitality and respect to the guest; and "respect" is one of the most important words in the Greek language.

Slow your pace down, take in the sights and sounds

However especially since the debt crisis, the Greeks show little respect when it comes to paying taxes: tavernas and cafés often expect guests to pay in cash with no bill supplied in order to evade paying heavy taxes. Above-board establishments will bring a bill to the table with your drinks or when you ask to pay. Tourists can also ***show respect*** to locals by discretely leaving a tip on the table when leaving the restaurant rather than giving it demonstratively to the waiter.

1000–500 BC Founding of the three Doric city states Líndos, Kámiros and Ialissós

490 BC Rhodes is forced to capitulate to the Persians

408 BC Rhodes is laid waste by the Athenians. The three city states merge to form Rhodes Town

164 BC Rhodes becomes Roman

395 AD After the split of the Roman Empire, Rhodes falls to Byzantium

1309–1522 Rule of the Knights of St John

Boredom? A day by the sea is the perfect cure at the beach in Kallithéa

party goers who chill out in between in the hammocks and beach huts provided. A holiday should always be an expression of "freedom", one of the most important words on the island.

Power nap on the beach in hammocks

Rhodes was only granted its freedom, or ***independence,*** in 1947. Up until then, it spent many years governed by foreign rulers, a state which many of the islanders believe they are experiencing again today: they cannot understand why the austerity measures, imposed on Greece by Europe and the rest of the world, mainly affect the little people. However, most Rhodians are better off than their neighbours in the big cities on the mainland. The cafés remain busy although guests tend to order less and are not as generous with their invitations as they used to be. You do not see poverty on the streets (or refugees either); the only indication of the island's hard times are the food donation boxes in the supermarkets. Rhodes has kept itself above water mainly thanks to tourism. Locals demonstrate their appreciation and gratitude by showing you their ***hospitality and kindness***.

WHAT'S HOT

1 Balancing act

An elevating affair Even the lethal cobbled streets in the Old Town of Rhodes do not stop local women wearing record high heels. High-heeled sandals are the latest craze. The Greek shoe trendsetter *Migato (Odós Ethn. Makaríou 31 | New Town)* keeps shoppers up with the latest fashions. If you prefer a more comfortable pair of sandals, head to the fashion-conscious Rhodes designer *Sojo Shoe Boutique (Odós Th. Dimiztríou 71–53 | New Town)* where all models are made in Greece.

2 A leaner option

Budget-saving vegetables In times of crisis, many Rhodians are living healthier by not eating meat. Only two restaurants in the Old Town have dared to convert over to vegetarian cuisine: the *To Maroúli (Odós Plátonos 12)* and the *Rubisco (Odós Sokratoús 67)*, yet increasingly more eateries offer meatless versions of traditional Greek dishes. Tomatoes and peppers are frequently stuffed with just rice and herbs and vine and cabbage leaves are prepared without mincemeat.

3 Vaping craze

Scents in the air They may not be healthy, but shishas, known here as *nargile*, can be found in many of the island's trendy cafés and beach bars, for example in *Bliss (Leofóros Kallithéas)* and in *Kafenes Fíli (Odós Amfitrítis 111)*. It is the perfect way to unwind with friends and companions. E-cigarettes have also exploded in popularity in Greece. The equipment required has become increasingly more exclusive and many shops now specialise in this craze, especially in the New Town of Rhodes.

There are lots of new things to discover on Rhodes. A few of the most interesting are listed below

Hyper, Hyper?

4

Techno vs. Entechno Careful: the words may be similar but techno music and entechno music couldn't be more different in sound. Both genres are currently in trend among young islanders. Entechno is a type of orchestrated folk sound with rock-style ballads sung in Greek and performed by a solo artist accompanied by a single guitar; a sound which certainly will not appeal to techno fans. The more famous Greek entechno artists include Giórgos Daláras *(www.dalaras.gr)* and Giánnis Haroúlis *(www.haroulis.eu)* who went on a European tour in 2017.

Aristotle forever

5

Colossal body art What has been a regular sight on British tourists for decades has now grown in popularity among island locals. More and more Rhodians, both men and women, are queuing up to get a tattoo. But instead of a British bulldog or Union Jack, the Greeks choose more traditional motifs such as Greek letters that do not exist in Latin script. Quotes from the philosopher Aristotle and Greek sayings are also among their favourites. "Your body is the canvas, we are the artists" is the advertising slogan of *House of Pain (Odós Amerikís 53 | New Town | on Facebook)*. The studio is only open until 11:30pm unlike *Mr. Painless (Odós Gríva 27 | New Town | on Facebook)* which is open all around the clock for those who pluck up the courage after a drink or two. His name sounds more appealing anyway...

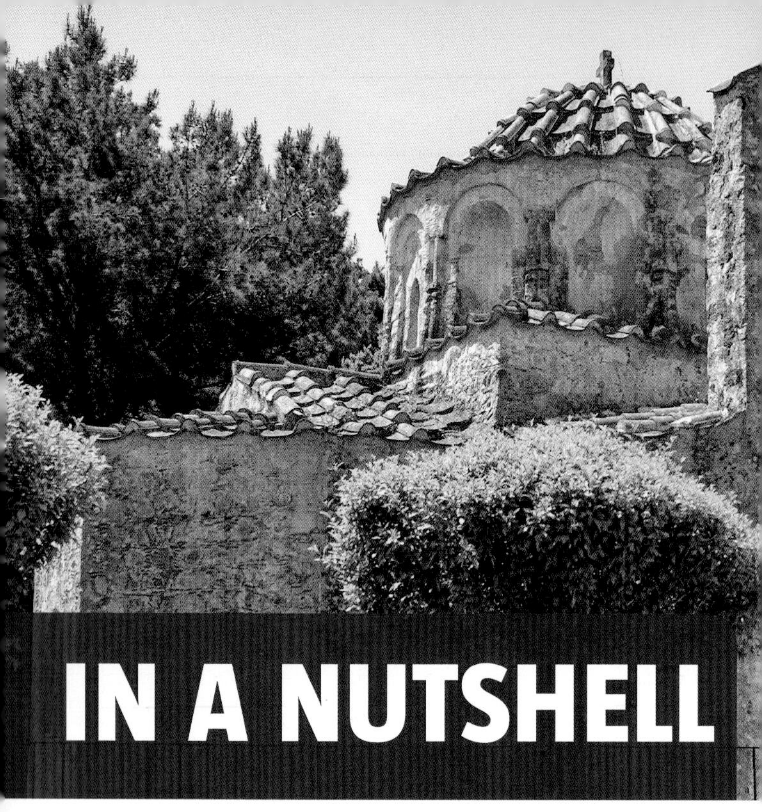

IN A NUTSHELL

ANIMAL WELFARE

Oh, how cute they are! And how amicable! Stray dogs and homeless cats are not a rare sight on Rhodes. The animals are harmless, but they have a hard life and go hungry, particularly in winter. The financial crisis has led to a number of pedigree dogs being abandoned in the wild or on refuse tips. Animal welfare societies on the island organise animal transports and adoptions overseas, for example *www.rhodesanimalwelfaresociety.gr.*

BANKS AND BUILDING BOOM

Before the country was declared bankrupt in 2010, many Greeks were living in a land of milk and honey. Their banks would call regularly encouraging them to take out credit. "What, only 20,000 euros? No, take 50,000 euros instead", the banks would say, knowing full well who owned what land and how much money their clients earned. New building developments were then proposed, making people believe they had sufficient financial means to invest. Many people unfortunately succumbed to temptation: the roads are full of large luxury limousines, SUVs and off-roaders as well as many unfinished buildings. The banks' generosity stopped as soon as the crisis hit. The Greeks are now in serious debt. The only compensation is that the banks cannot find buyers for houses they want to auction. The only profit is to be made from luxury proper-

 Photo: Ágios Nikólaos Fountoúkli chapel

Background info at a glance – to help you get to know the sunny Greek island and its people, the Rhodians, better

ties going for prices above 1 million euros. However, there is hope on the horizon: foreigners currently living under the Erdogan regime are looking increasingly for property on Rhodes.

BEACH FOR EVERYONE

All of Rhodes beaches are open to the public free of charge – although they can be state-leased for private purposes as a result of the crisis. Not all of the beaches are packed with sun loungers and parasols and you are welcome to spread your towel out anywhere. Beach tavernas and bars line the promenades and water sports facilities can be found in all major resorts between mid-May and mid-October. Lifeguards are a seldom sight on beaches due to the lack of funding from the local councils.

BYZANTINE

Do you like to understand what you read? You will encounter the word "Byzantine" on thousands of brown signs dotted all over Rhodes. The Byzantine era

Irony of fate: The God of Sun, Helios, the Colossus of Rhodes, was melted down

was the continuation of the Roman Empire in the East from around 500 to 1453, roughly the same period as our Middle Ages. Until 1309, Rhodes belonged to the Byzantine Empire. This Empire spread across all of Asia Minor, the Balkans and Greece. Its capital city was Constantinople which was renamed as Istanbul when it fell to the Ottoman Turks in 1453. Many Greeks would like to see a return to this period which is why the yellow and black Byzantine flag can be seen flying in front of many churches and monasteries on Rhodes. The island also serves as the residence for the Orthodox Patriarch, the equivalent of the Catholic Pope.

COLOSSAL

What a colossal man! One of the Seven Wonders of the World, cast in bronze between 294 and 282 BC and 33 m (108 ft) high, it stood astride the harbour entrance or on the Acropolis high above the town. Only fifty years later, it was destroyed by an earthquake. The bronze was melted down and not a single piece was preserved. However the Colossus of Rhodes is present everywhere on the island today, with souvenirs ranging from metal statues to prop up the book shelf, colourful postcards to sunbathing towels.

CRISIS MANAGEMENT

Krísis? What crisis? Most island inhabitants see the crisis, which erupted in Greece in 2010, as a chronic illness from which the country may never recover. Salaries, pensions and the minimum wage have all been cut while taxes rose considerably. Youth unemployment has reached over 50 percent while the country's general rate of unemployment has exceeded 20 percent– and there are no real signs of recovery. Even a radical incision (i.e. debt relief) will not prevent this patient surviving off the euro cash lifeline from its European neighbours. The people on Rhodes have adapted their lifestyle accordingly. They are planting vegetables instead of ornamental shrubs, only ordering what they can eat in tavernas, buying smaller cars and have stopped building new houses.

They also give each other a helping hand rather than relying on day workers from Eastern Europe. As long as the tourists keep coming, they will manage to survive.

EARLY EU

700 years ago, something like the EU already existed – and its capital was not Brussels, but Rhodes. In the state of the Order of the Knights of St John, Christians from many European countries lived together peacefully and voted their ruler for a lifetime. It did not matter much where you were born. Instead, everyone was organized according to "tongues", which were something like "languages" at the time.

FAUX AMI

"Nee" in Greek is a faux ami for speakers of many European languages. Greeks say the "nee" word when they get married for example and it simply means "yes". The commonly used word "entáxi" is another cause for confusion. No, the Greeks don't want to travel by taxi all the time despite their lack of funds: they are simply saying "okay".

GREEN – THE COLOUR OF HOPE

Although the Greeks recognise the importance of protecting the environment, the country simply does not have the resources. With no incineration plant and thankfully no nuclear power plant, the island relies on two normal power stations, an old one near Sorόni and a new one near Prassoníssi, both of which burn crude oil. Alternative forms of energy have had mixed success. When a developer went bankrupt, many private investors on Rhodes lost a lot of money and locals are now understandably sceptical to invest in solar parks. Wind energy is not exploited enough. The only sector where Rhodes has gained ground is in its use of solar panels. They can be seen on many hotel roofs and private residences and show that the average citizen can make very good savings by going green.

HARPOONS

"Kamáki" translates literally as harpoon. What it means is Casanova and is practically a profession in Rhodes. Adorned with gold chains and big rings, young men and older playboys try to court and conquer female tourists on holiday. They see themselves as irresistible and are organized in private clubs. The kamáki men are unique to Rhodes and a documentary film "Colossi of Love" even reported on this phenomena. They keep a list of their successes: who managed to court the most women and the most nationalities? They are not troublesome and they will leave anyone alone who is obviously not interested in their "services". The womanizers see themselves as athletes and stick to "fair play" rules.

IN BEST COMPANY

People on Rhodes do not like spending time on their own. A cosy twosome is reserved for a certain hour of the day. Otherwise Greeks prefer a *paréa;* a group of friends or acquaintances, who regularly meet up to drink coffee or eat, go to the disco and on holiday together. The question asked by friends afterwards is not what the hotel or food was like but how the *paréa* was. In case you do have to go it alone, you will always be accompanied by the island's saints. They are present as icons wherever you go on the island – whether in the car, in the ticket booth or in the open fields – either as printed images or painted on church and chapel walls and hanging on the sides of the road. You know you are always in safe hands and in good company.

KOMBOLOIA

The *komboloi,* or worry beads, are often seen on old men and in souvenir shops. Although it resembles a Catholic rosary, it is a variation of the Turkish prayer beads. The Greeks adopted their own style of bead for relaxation, enjoyment and generally passing the time. The *kómbos,* or knot used to hold the beads together, is regarded as a lucky charm. Apparently it also helps to quit smoking.

LAND OF CONFUSION

People from Rhodes hate strict rules and are quite liberal where their spelling is concerned; a custom which can confuse many a tourist. In Greek, place names can be written differently on signs and maps while the Latin spelling is even more haphazard. "Agia" meaning "Saint" is a good example. It is sometimes written as "Agia" (as in the Marco Polo guides) or "Aghia" or even "Ayia". All three spellings are accepted and combined as the Greeks please. Where there are no rules, there are fewer mistakes.

NO HURRY

Do you know what tomorrow will bring? The Rhodians certainly don't know and don't waste their time planning for the long term. Large events and festivals are only made public a few days in advance while timetables or the opening times of museums or excavation sites are posted online at short notice. Vague arrangements to meet the following morning, afternoon, evening or even next week are made, adding the all-important "ta leme" – "we'll talk again later." You can then expect a call one hour beforehand to confirm the exact time – give or take the customary half an hour.

TÁVLI

Two men sit at a table, a board, two dice and chunky plastic tokens between them, their heads bowed, muscles taut – do not disturb! *Távli* is much more than just the Greek version of backgammon. It's an essential part of the life of the traditionally-minded Greek male and many a young Greek woman as are the car keys and the mobile phone on the table. You can rent the board game in almost every cafe and many bars. Just google the rules!

THE NEIGHBOURS TO VISIT

For a long time, NATO's partner Turkey was the archenemy of many Greeks. Although ties improved considerably in the 1990s, the relationship has gradually deteriorated since the refugee crisis and Er-

Life takes place at the beach on Rhodes – for example here on the Anthony Quinn Bay

dogan's threat to Turkish democracy. This situation does not change the fact that day trippers from Turkey have been the blessing in disguise for bar and restaurant owners on Rhodes. The Turkish like to dine in style just like the Greeks did before the economic crisis and unlike many Europeans order far more than just a Greek salad. They also appreciate traditional Greek music and enjoy live performances. They even employ the services of an interpreter to translate the lyrics. The sounds are familiar to them – Rhodian folk songs have strong oriental influences.

WEBSITES ARE YESTERDAY'S NEWS

Although websites on Rhodes are usually creative in design, they often lack up-to-date information and news. Admittedly it's hard work maintaining a homepage which is why many of the restaurant and café owners have switched to Facebook & co for posting events and live acts. Hoteliers prefer to pay commission fees to hotel booking portals rather than engaging the services of professional web agencies. More and more private Facebook, Instagram and Linkedin accounts are also being created. Simply enter "Rhodes", "rodos" or "rhodos" into your browser and the "loading more results" seems endless.

WORLD OF WONDERS

Could you sometimes need a helping hand in times of trouble? Do as the locals do and make the sign of the cross on your chest (fold your thumb and first two fingers down against the base of your thumb, holding your ring and small finger together and then move your hand up-down-right and left) and whisper your wish to the appointed Saint. Christóphoros grants a safe journey by land, Nikólaos protects seafarers and Fanoúrios is called upon to find lost persons and objects. The Virgin Mary, the *Panagía,* can help in all situations.

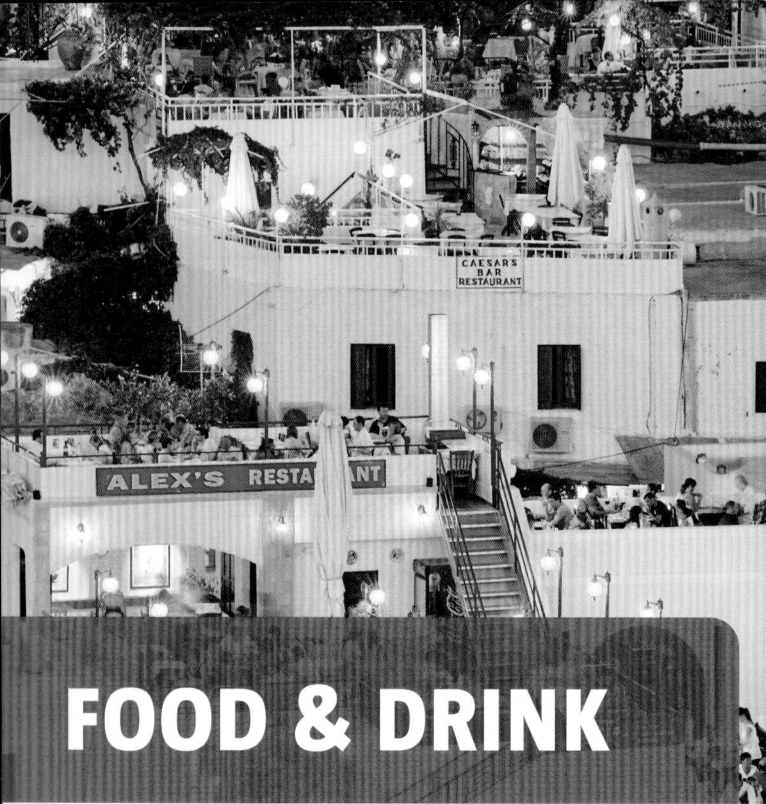

FOOD & DRINK

You can eat Gyros and Tzatziki at home in your local Greek restaurant. Be adventurous on Rhodes and try some of the unknown Greek specialities and exotic dishes from other continents.

Mediterranean cuisine, along French and Italian lines, is en vogue; ***exotic restaurants*** with Indian, Japanese and Mexican food are competing fiercely with the established ones, especially in the capital. Young Greek chefs and restaurant and bar owners are holding their own by returning to the best traditional style of ***cooking from their grandmothers' day*** and giving it a creative make-over, using largely fresh, regional produce. Greeks love to have a great variety of different dishes on the table at one time. They seldom go out alone for dinner in the evening, though, as eating in company is preferable to a cosy dinner for two. The Hellenes consider the ***company of friends and relatives at the table***, collectively known as the ***paréa***, to be just as important as the culinary experience. The diners always order plenty of different dishes which are placed in the centre of the table. Each person takes as much as they like of whatever they fancy. Usually there will be meat and fish served up on large platters, and everyone helps themselves. Traditionally, more food is ordered than can possibly be eaten: to eat everything is not "the done thing", as it would be a sign of obviously having ordered too little. All plates, even the empty ones, remain on the table. The waiter does not clear them

 Photo: Terraced restaurants in Líndos

Regional and cosmopolitan at the same time – the island's gastro scene is lively and full of first-class highlights

away, so that everyone can see how well the *paréa* has dined.

You can best enjoy the whole spectrum of Greek cooking if, like the locals themselves, you order a ***variety of starters***, rather than choosing a traditional menu as you would elsewhere in Europe. You can often even do without a main course. These so-called ***mesédes*** include various purées and thick sauces which the Greeks designate as salads. Current favourites are also croquettes made of different vegetables, also from squid, puréed fish roe and potato *(taramá)* or your common or garden chicken. The potato patties or mashed chickpeas rolled into balls are delicious. The turnovers, or *píttes,* made of puff pastry and filled with cheese and/or spinach, sausage or meat, are a traditional favourite. Fried slices of aubergine or courgettes also count as *mesédes*, as do fresh salads, pickled fish, anchovies, olives, oven-baked cheese and seafood. When it comes to main courses, Greek

LOCAL SPECIALITIES

FAJITÓ (FOOD)

briám – Ratatouille with plenty of aubergines and olive oil
chtapódi – Octopus, either grilled, boiled or served cold
dolmádes – Stuffed vine leaves, mostly served hot in an egg-lemon sauce (photo right)
fáva – Puréed yellow split peas
jemistés – Peppers, courgettes and/or tomatoes stuffed with rice and mincemeat
juvétsi – Noodles resembling grains of rice, cooked in a clay dish in the oven with beef or lamb
kakaviá – Fish soup where guests select the fish. It is cooked in fish stock, but served separately
ksifía – Fried or grilled swordfish steak
marídes – Deep-fried anchovies
paidákia – Lamb chops, usually from the charcoal grill
revithókeftédes – A kind of patty or croquette made of mashed chickpeas
stifádo – Usually beef, sometimes rabbit, stew in tomato-cinnamon sauce with braised onions
supjés – A kind of *kalamáres,* unlike the latter, though, always fresh and never frozen

POTÁ (DRINKS)

frappé – Cold, frothy instant coffee
retsína – White or rosé wine flavoured with the resin of the Aleppo pine (photo left)
soúma – Rhodian variation on what is known elsewhere in Greece as *rakí* or *tsípouro* – spirit distilled from the remains of grapes after pressing

chefs are less imaginative. If their compatriots go out to eat they want ***meat and fish from the charcoal grill***. Accompanying sauces are rare – at best there will be a mixture of good olive oil and lemon to go with the fish. Jacket potatoes or potatoes roasted in the oven are becoming more popular, but the usual side dishes are more or less poor cousins to standard chips. ***Dishes cooked in the oven*** are a traditional highlight in Greek cuisine. Everyone has heard of the famous casseroles topped with béchamel sauce, such as *moussaká* (aubergines and mincemeat) or *pastítsjo* (macaroni and mincemeat). Baked aubergines, lamb baked in the oven with potatoes *(kleftikó)* or *exochikó*, lamb baked in foil with vegetables, are all delicious.

Rhodian ***desserts have a touch of the Orient*** about them. You'll rarely find them on the menu at a restaurant; you have to go instead to a *zacharoplastío*, the Greek equivalent of a cake or pastry shop. There are plenty of these, but outside Rhodes Town they seldom offer somewhere to sit down. Local residents usually take their cakes home with them. The best place to indulge your sweet tooth is to trawl around the pastry shops on the harbour side of the Néa Agorá market in Rhodes Town. The often colourful creamy cakes and gateaux are a delight to look at. However, the apple cakes, ***milópitta***, and walnut cakes, ***karidópitta,*** are considered as more typically Greek. Both can be enjoyed with ice-cream, which also goes well with the oriental-style pastries, such as *baklavás* and *kataífi,* eaten with a knife and dessert fork. Traditionally a speciality of Northern Greece, the *bougátsa* is a turnover made of strudel dough and filled either with vanilla custard or sheep's cheese.

In the more traditional villages and in towns, most ***tavernas*** are open from 9 o'clock in the morning until midnight. The Greeks eat wherever and whenever they fancy, and not when the landlord decides. Lunch is often eaten as late as 2 or 3 o'clock in the afternoon, and it is common to get together with your *paréa* – your friends or relatives – at 10 or 11 o'clock at night.

The island's favourite hot beverage is ***coffee*** in its many different variations. Whether traditional mocha, *kafés ellinikós,* instant or filter coffee, espresso and cappuccino served hot or cold – you must always say how sweet you want it because the ground coffee is mixed with sugar and then brewed. You also need to order the milk separately for espresso, instant and filter coffee.

Whisky is the Greeks' favourite spirit, yet the traditional ***ouzo***, made of aniseed, is widespread. In rural areas, people like to drink ***soúma***, distilled from the remains of grapes after pressing and similar to an Italian grappa. To accompany your meal, you are served water, wine or beer, which is often available on draught. ***Wines*** from the island's major wineries Cair and Emery are available everywhere. Lovers of rarer varieties of wine should ask for something from the Rhodian winery Tríantáfillou or from Ktíma Papaioánnou and Ktíma Mércouri on the Peloponnese.

Decaffeinated? No thanks! Coffee is the life blood of many islanders

SHOPPING

Rhodes is a good money-saving destination. You can find a new summer outfit and a fashionable accessory, culinary specialities to take back home and the usual kitsch for your relatives. The best places to shop are in Rhodes City and Líndos.

CERAMICS

To this day, Rhodes has been an island of potters. You'll find a large number of potters' studios and showrooms on the road between Faliráki and Líndos, particularly around Archángelos. The colourful enamelled wall plates are typical of Rhodes.

CULINARY TREATS

Rhodian wine, liqueurs and Rhodian ouzo may still be transported home in your flight baggage. Pickled olives, herbs, pistachios, coffee or honey conjure up the tastes and smells of the sunny island on your dining table.

FASHION

You can buy Versace & co. anywhere in the world – but the creations of Greek designers are sold exclusively in Hellas, for example in the Old Town of Rhodes and in Líndos.

JEWELLERY & ACCESSORIES

Only a few jewellers actually produce at least part of their collections themselves. Much comes from the Greek mainland, some is manufactured overseas.

LEATHER GOODS

As animal fur has become taboo in most cultures, the island's furriers have had to adapt accordingly. Some have focused on Eastern European tourists while the rest have converted to leather production. The prices cannot compete with the Turkish, and the design is not up to Italian standards which is why most of the leather is imported from the two countries. There is only one small workshop in the Old Town which still makes its own sandals, handbags and belts.

MUSIC

There are a host of Greek music DVDs available. If you're looking for quality, it's best to buy in shops and not from the

Sunshine to go – thyme, ouzo and marinated olives are a piece of Rhodes you can take home with you

frequently encountered hawkers. What's more, in the shops you get the chance to listen to a couple of tracks before you buy. Alongside popular artists such as Míkis Theodorákis and Mános Chatzidákis, their fellow musicians Jórgos Daláras, María Farandoúri and Háris Alexíou are by no means one-hit wonders.

NATURAL SPONGES

Traditional ships operate as stores for mussels from all over the world at the harbour in Emborikó Limáni. Cheap goods usually come from the Caribbean; sponges from the nearby Greek island of Kálimnos, on the other hand, are more expensive.

SHOES

Women on Rhodes are of an adventurous kind. They like bright colours and unusual shapes and their heels are murderously high. You can also find all kinds of trainers and sandals. Most of the shoe shops are located in the New Town.

SOUVENIRS FROM TURKEY

Day-trippers should be aware of the customs regulations when returning to Greece. The following limits apply: 40 cigarettes or 50 g of tobacco, 1 l of spirits (over 22 % vol.) or 2 l (under 22 % vol.), plus items for personal use to the value of 430 euros (children under 15 years up to 150 euros).

UMBRELLAS

The sun may shine at most times of the year but Rhodes is still the world's capital for umbrellas. Virtually no tourist leaves Rhodes without buying an umbrella first. You can find everything from a three euros umbrella to designer items. Most stores are situated around the *Platía Kyprou* (see p. 43) in the New Town.

RHODES TOWN

MAP INSIDE THE BACK COVER (119 F2) (H5) **It's all a question of taste but Rhodes is arguably one of the prettiest cities in the world. There's no doubt though that its Old Town is the best preserved city of its size.**

The capital city of "Rodos" has been a site of uninterrupted settlement for 2400 years which makes history come alive in this unique and vibrant place. Outside its 4 km/2.5 miles long city wall, Rhodes Town (pop. 51,000) has even more to attract visitors including oriental-style buildings and a long-stretching beach with views over to the Turkish coastline.

The centuries have left their mark on the Old Town. Mosques and minarets, churches and a synagogue show that multiculturalism is not a modern, urban invention. The 2000-year old remains of ancient walls are testimony to the monumental architectural achievement in a period where most other Europeans were still living in caves and huts. 500-year old houses are now used as small boutique hotels and guesthouses, cocktail bars and tavernas. The main streets through the Old Town resemble a bustling bazaar while the winding side lanes are populated by more cats than people. The Avenue of the Knights is one of the world's best preserved medieval streets – and the Archaeological Museum was once the most modern hospitals of its time.

Once Rhodes' naval port, Mandráki now has rows and rows of excursion boats and yachts anchored here. The neighbouring port in front of the mighty city walls is

 Photo: View over the town and the Palace of the Grand Masters

A journey into the past, but not a boring one – more than 2000 years of history come alive in the alleyways of the island's capital

CITY **WHERE TO START?**
Ideally, visit the capital by bus or taxi, since parking spaces are rare. The bus station is directly behind the **Néa Agorá**, just a few steps from the Old Town and Mandráki Harbour. If you do decide to go by car, you're most likely to find a reasonably priced parking space between Mandráki Harbour, the Town Hall and the Aquarium.

where fishing boats, fast passenger catamarans and enormous cruise liners dock. To the west, the New Town stretches along two beaches and is full of modern shops, bars, pubs and hotels. This is where tourists come to party while the young Greeks prefer to chill out in the Old Town until sunrise.

SIGHTSEEING

ÁGIOS FANOÚRIOS (122 C5)
Have you forgotten or lost something? Greeks in this case call on the help of Saint

Fanoúrios. According to many devout Hellenes, he works better than any lost property office. The ancient church in the city is also dedicated to this patron saint of lost belongings and has its origins in the 9th century. This can be seen clearly below the

The "crouching Aphrodite" in the Museum of Archaeology

ground level of the present structure dating back to the Crusader period. Between the sooty frescoes from the 13th to 15th century, you can well imagine how people used to gather here in candlelight. *Open in the daytime | Odós Agíou Fanoúriou*

OLD TOWN ★

MAP ON P. 122/123

RRecently voted the number one world heritage site by UNESCO, the Old Town of Rhodes catapults you back 2500 years into history. It is impossible to lose your way: the city is fully enclosed by its 4 km/2.5 miles long *city wall.* You can either walk on top of the wall or in its 2.5 km/1.5 mile long *moat* skirting inland (see p. 39). The best way to find your bearings around the Old Town is by following the main streets and then explore the quieter corners walking in a zig-zag direction. Buildings erected by the Byzantines, Crusaders, Israelites, Ottoman Turks and Greeks are embedded in the ancient fortifications. There is no new building to spoil the view. Yet despite its antiquity, holidaymakers from around the world give this city its cosmopolitan flair. It's also fun to watch them marching down the cobblestone catwalks past the many street cafés and tavernas.

MUSEUM OF ARCHAEOLOGY ★

(122 C3)

The island's most significant museum lures even the most reluctant visitor to spend more than an hour inside because it is far more than just an exhibition space. Surrounded by beautiful gardens, the two-storey building itself is a perfect photo opportunity, overlooking a large courtyard with a pile of cannon balls and an ancient marble lion. Its finest treasure is a small marble Aphrodite statue depicting two women with beautifully sculpted figures. However the tour begins by following the 28-step open staircase up to the first-floor arcade. Walk through the largest doorway to enter a long, high-ceilinged room from the 15th century: the sick and the injured were treated in this room by the Knights of Saint John when the building served as a hospital. The gravestones on the wall are in memory of those who couldn't be saved. A small door leads into the dining halls where the two Aphrodite statues now stand. Heralded as a masterpiece of Greek classicism, the tomb stele

depicts Krito and Timarista (around 410 BC), a young woman who is mourning the loss of her dead mother.
Now continue along a terrace with more sculptures out into the gardens where beautiful ancient mosaics are exhibited in an open-air foyer. One of the mosaics depicts a centaur, half horse, half man, returning from the hunt with its prey, a scrawny looking rabbit, hanging from its mouth. From the gardens, visitors can walk around two other special exhibitions concentrating on Rhodes in the Minoan and Mycenaean period around 2nd century BC. Stairs lead up to the upper arcade to twelve side rooms which mainly hold painted ceramics found in Rhodes dating between 500 BC and 500 AD. When you leave the museum and turn left, you reach another museum room which is only accessible from the street. The room showcases enormous pottery vessels once used to bury the dead in a squatting position. They couldn't have found it too uncomfortable. *Approx. Easter–Oct daily 8am–8pm, Nov–Easter Tue–Sun 8:30am–2.40pm; special exhibitions April–Oct only daily 9am–4.50pm | admission Easter–Oct 8 euros, Nov–Easter 4 euros | Odós Apéllou | Old Town*

PALACE OF THE GRAND MASTERS ★ ● (122 B2)

The most photographed and visited sight in the Old Town is in fact a fake. The Italians reconstructed the Palace of the Grand Master in the early 1930s to suit the tastes of the megalomaniac dictator Mussolini. It was planned to be his residence if he ever came to live on the island but he was too busy masterminding wars and stayed in Rome.
Only a few parts of the original structure remain, including the monumental entrance portal with its impressive towers.

MARCO POLO HIGHLIGHTS

★ Old Town
Every stone and every building within the medieval city walls is worth a look → p. 34

★ Museum of Archaeology
Ancient treasures displayed in an old medieval hospital → p. 34

★ Palace of the Grand Masters
Quite a sight – whichever way you look at it → p. 35

★ Mandráki Harbour
The finest harbour on the entire island → p. 36

★ Néa Agorá
Get together at the market hall – any time of the day → p. 38

★ Odós Sokratoús
Named after the famous philosopher, the street in the Old Town is lined with interesting stores → p. 38

★ Avenue of the Knights
Follow the street paved with pebbles back to Crusader times → p. 39

★ Filérimos
The mountain with ancient ruins and a romantic monastery offers a bird's-eye view on Rhodes → p. 47

★ Kallithéa Thermal Baths
Splash around in the historic ambience of these unique thermal springs → p. 48

Not to be found in any DIY store – ancient mosaic tiles in the Palace of the Grand Masters

The building's interior was completely redesigned with ancient mosaics from the island of Kos, old solid wood furnishings and Chinese porcelain – elements unknown to the Order of the Knights of St John, whose Grand Master resided here from the late 14th century to 1522. The building lost its importance when the Turks invaded who used the hospital as an army barracks and prison, the palace's church as a cowshed and the neighbouring church of the Order as an arsenal. In 1856, a bolt of lightning triggered an explosion blowing up the church and turned the original Palace into a mass of ruins. The ground floor hosts two exhibitions. From a historical perspective, these exhibits are far more valuable than the actual building and upper-floor rooms. One is dedicated to Byzantine Rhodes from the 4th century to 1522. The second, more interesting exhibit is Rhodes 2400, showcasing recent archaeological findings. And because archaeologists tend to dig faster than they write, many of these sensational objects have not yet been listed and therefore cannot be photographed, nor can you buy postcards of them. *April–Oct daily 8am–8pm, Nov–March Tue–Sun 8:30am–2.40pm; special exhibitions April–Oct only, daily 9am–4.40pm | admission April–Oct 6 euros, Nov–March 3 euros | Platía Kleovoúlou*

MANDRÁKI HARBOUR ★ (122 C1)

The question on everyone's lips is "where did the famous Colossus of Rhodes once stand?" Nobody knows for sure. Legend would have you believe it stood astride the entrance to Mandráki Harbour precisely where two pillars are now erected carrying the island's heraldic animals, the stag and the doe, *elafós* and *elafína*. Mandráki is the central hub of the city. Where's the tourist information office? In Mandráki. Where's the market? In Mandráki. Where do the boats depart? In Mandráki. Translated into English, Mandráki means "small sheepfold". No one knows exactly how the ancient military port of Rhodes Town got its current name. One possible explanation is that the name could have something to do with its physical structure: Mandráki Harbour resembles a pair of pincers and encircles the ships rather like the fold does the herd of sheep. It's well worth a stroll around this picturesque harbour: the jetty with its three windmills and the harbour fortress *Ágios Nikólaos* all date from the 15th century.

Mandráki designates not only the harbour itself, but also the district behind it.

A constant source of fascination, Mandráki gives you a taste of maritime flair, the hustle and bustle of a market and the buzz of city life. Of course, this gem has many admirers, so on some days, so many that they tread on each other's toes at the Eleftherías (Liberty) Gate, the shortest way to the Old Town. This is partly due to the fact that cars also pass through the gate, leaving only a narrow strip on either side for pedestrians. But, the ● fishermen who cast their lines from the pier take their time.

MONTE SMITH (U A6)

Like every Greek city with its origins in antiquity, Rhodes Town has its own Acropolis. Unfortunately, little remains of its temples. A visit to the 110-m/360 ft-high hill is still worthwhile, however, as you can view the entire town from above: old and new, beautiful and ugly. Its present, rather incongruous name comes from the commander of the British fleet which was stationed on Rhodes in the early 19th century. The fleet was supposed to police the eastern Mediterranean and protect it from possible attack by the forces of Napoleon who was engaged in a campaign against Egypt at the time. The Italians gave the hill the name *Monte Santo Stefano,* which is still occasionally used today. It lies in the west of the town and can be reached easily by bus. Three-and-a-half columns of a temple dedicated to Apollo make up the sparse remains. Furthermore, a reconstructed theatre and a partially rebuilt

Mandráki harbour is the atmospheric centre point of the town

● stadium are waiting to be explored. The track is exactly 201 m (220 yd) long. It dates to the second century BC and was almost completely reconstructed by the Italians. How about a sprint? *Permanently accessible via Odós Voríou Ipírou (New Town) | bus No. 5 from Mandráki/ Néa Agorá*

MUSEUM OF MODERN GREEK ART

In the *Art Gallery* (122 C2) *(Platía Símis 2)* and in the *New Art Gallery* (U B1) *(Platía Charitou | both Tue–Sat 9am–2pm)* there are displays of Greek art from the 19th and 20th centuries. Rhodes has yet to produce any masters. *Admission 3 euros, valid for both exhibitions*

NÉA AGORÁ ★ ● (122 B–C1)

You cannot overlook this building: it has seven corners, but is only one-and-a-half storeys high. Under the arcades facing the harbour, there are a number of cafés that are busy till late at night. Here, you'll find sweets such as *baklavás* and *kataífi,* originally from Turkey and now extremely popular on Rhodes, too. Two kiosks between the cafés sell international newspapers and magazines. Inside the Néa Agorá stands the former fish market hall, recognisable only by the fine fish reliefs on the capitals of its columns. Two kafenía and several grill restaurants are much in demand, particularly during the day. *Platía Eleftherías Mandráki*

ODÓS SOKRATOÚS (SOCRATES STREET) ★ (122/123 B–D 2–4)

Shopping is on the agenda when you arrive at Socrates Street, the main street running through the Old Town. The street climbs gently uphill from the Platía Ippokrátous at the bottom to the Mosque of Süleyman at the top end. The street is lined on both sides with shops selling all the usual souvenirs and more besides: jewellery and freshly roasted coffee, leather and furs, natural cosmetics and Greek culinary specialities, kitsch, t-shirts and even lightweight knight armoury. Standing at a slight angle halfway down the street is the tiny *Mehmet Aga Mosque.* The island's oldest coffee house stands diagonally opposite the mosque and is waiting for a new tenant. From here, you head up the street to the pink-coloured *Mosque of Süleyman* at the top end. Dating from the 19th century, the mosque no longer holds acts of worships (not open to the public). Opposite is the tiny *Turkish Library (April–Oct Mon–Sat 9am–3pm | free admission)* built in the 18th century. The library contains Turkish, Persian and Arabic manuscripts and books depicting an Islamic culture without religious wars and terrorism.

PLATÍA ARIÓNOS (122 B4)

This tiny square with mosque and large *Turkish baths* was a hive of activity in Ottoman times. Today the square is fre-

Want a view? Then head up to the centuries-old city walls

quented mainly by locals who come in the evenings to relax in the three music cafés. *Old Town*

PLATÍA DORIÉOS (122 C5)

Three bars and a minaret can be found on this square. The bars serve mainly salads, burgers and pizzas with views of the *Rejab Pascha Mosque* which has been waiting 15 years for a renovation. This is a perfect place for a light lunch break. *Old Town*

AVENUE OF THE KNIGHTS ★ (122 B–C3)

The Odós Ippotón is the only late medieval residential street in Europe which has remained fully intact. It runs in a perfectly straight line from the hospital of the Order of St John, which now houses the Museum of Archaeology, to the Palace of the Grand Masters. To the left and right stand the inns of the various tongues of the Order (see "Early EU", p. 22), decorated with the heraldic emblems of each Grand Master. The finest belonged to the French knights and stands almost in the centre. *Permanently accessible; building interiors cannot be viewed | Odós Ippotón | Old Town*

CITY WALLS AND MOAT (U C–E 4–6)

Towering over the city's harbour, the fortifications of Rhodes were undeniably an intimidating sight to Turkish soldiers who invaded in 1522. Their mission to conquer the city probably seemed downright impossible. Indeed, the siege lasted six months and the besiegers had to resort to starving the city's inhabitants. The knights finally surrendered and withdrew from the island. A stroll through the deep, very wide ● moat will give you an impression of the colossal task facing the Ottoman invaders *(main entrances on the Platía Riminis* (U C4) *and the Pylí Arkadía* (U E5) *| freely accessible)*. Kleine Fitness-Einlage unterwegs: VersTry for fun just lifting one of the many stone cannon balls which are lying around the rampart. Now for a change of perspective: climb up the city walls

(April–Oct Mon–Fri 10am–3pm | admission 3 euros; tickets at the Palace of the Grand Masters) and look down along the moat. Dizzying! Sturdy shoes and surefootedness are essential if you want to walk along the accessible part of the 4 km/2.5 miles-long wall. Your reward: a great view over roofs and minarets of the Old Town, which already in 1988 has been declared a Unesco World Heritage Site.

KAHAL SHALOM SYNAGOGUE ● (122 E5)

The synagogue, built in 1577 and destroyed by the Germans in 1943, has been renovated and now functions as a Jewish museum and place of worship open to visitors of all religions. Members of the remaining Jewish community are on hand to answer questions. *May–Oct Sun–Fri 10am–3pm | free admission | Odós Dosiádou*

INSIDER TIP TURKISH CEMETERY (U C2)

It may seem like an unlikely place to relax and unwind but the city's old Turkish cemetery is a perfect retreat. An old Muslim woman, whose children have left the island to work in Turkey, looks after the forlorn cemetery and is always pleased to receive a small donation. The cemetery is in the shady grounds of the tiny *Mosque of Murad Reis* and the *Villa Cleobolus* where Lawrence Durrell lived in the 1940s, writing *Reflections on a Marine Venus.* The shady trees offer a perfect spot to lie down and rest for a while. *Accessible during the day | access from the Platía Koundourióti | New Town*

PROMENADE (U C2–3)

The city's ample promenade is called *Eleftherías,* meaning "Freedom". Its splendour and beauty unfortunately owe much to the Italian fascists who ruled over the island from 1912 to 1943 and their architectural legacy is still evident today. They erected classical buildings for example, the Bank of Greece, the Post Office, the Harbour Master's Office, the Town Hall and the city theatre inside the fortifications and the Governor's and Bishop's Palace facing the sea. They were also responsible for the construction of the Orthodox ● *Evangelismós* church *(daily 7am–noon and 5pm–7:30pm).* Formerly the main church of the Knights of St John, it was reconstructed according to old drawings in 1925 and its large walls inside are painted in traditional Byzantine style.

LUXURY IN THE FACE OF CRISIS

Rhodes has many celebrity fans – the Pink Floyd guitarist David Gilmour owned a luxury villa near Péfki for over 30 years and American legend Anthony Quinn also lived on the island. Rhodes is a popular retreat for those who can afford it. Prices of exclusive holiday homes have not plummeted despite the economic crisis and the demand for property is rising, mainly due to the growing unpopularity of Turkey's Erdogan government. Profiting from this, Rhodes and the Greek government expect record numbers of visitors and property hunters. Take a look at what is on offer: *www.engelvoelkers.com/en-gr/rhodes/.* By the way, David Gilmour sold his property on *www.luxuryestate.com.*

CLOCK TOWER (122 B3)

It is well worth climbing the tower to take in the fabulous view over the roofs and towers of the Old Town. *May–Oct daily 9am–11pm | admission (incl. a refreshing drink) 5 euros | Odós Orféos 1 | Old Town*

The clock tower and minaret of the Süleyman mosque will help you keep your bearings

FOOD & DRINK

INSIDER TIP AKTAÍON ● (122 B1)

Housed in the former casino for Italian officers, this café-restaurant with its tree-shaded terrace belongs to the town and is the meeting place of cultured local clientele. The location also attracts families with young children due to the childcare facilities in the bouncy castle next door. It has a large selection of cakes to choose from and its tasty dishes are served in large portions. Prices are moderate since the café depends on its regular customers. *Daily 8am–midnight | Platía Eleftherías | New Town | tel. 22 41 07 30 55*

DINÓRIS (122 C3)

The restaurant specialises in fish and seafood in all variations. An additional bonus is that at Dinóris, you dine in a lovely historic building dating to around 1300 in a hall that once served as a stable for the knights. Two specials with fish are offered at lunch with a glass of wine at a good price. *Platía Mousío 14a | Old Town | tel. 22 41 02 58 24 | www.dinoris.com | Expensive*

KON TIKI (122 C1)

Relaxation for your body and soul on board the Kontiki, a classy, two-storey floating restaurant located in the Mandráki Harbour. Enjoy a coffee, ice cream, sundowner or dinner accompanied by the sounds of waves on the Mediterranean. The food is inspired by Mediterranean and Japanese cooking with both eel and urchins on the menu. The view past the ship's mast to the fortifications, Palace of the Grand Masters and Néa Agorá is spectacular. *Daily from 10am | Mandráki | New Town | tel. 22 41 03 08 26 | www.kontiki.com.gr | Expensive*

INSIDER TIP KOÚKOS ● (U B2) (🗺)

This multi-faceted café-restaurant is also a pub with live music. It looks a bit like the set of a Greek film with its differently decorated areas. It offers a variety of food at reasonable prices. Opened year-round, this restaurant also has its own bakery where you can buy baked goods to takeaway. *Odós Mandilára 20 | tel. 22 41 07 30 22 | Moderate*

INSIDER TIP **MAMA SOFIA** ● (122 B3)
Mama Sofia, who opened this restaurant in 1967, is still running the eatery and arrives at 6am every day to prepare the food, chat with the cleaning ladies and cook some of the desserts. At 4pm she leaves the business in the hands of her two sons Stávros and Jánnis, her grandson Sotíris, his Japanese wife and Alex from Albania. Together they provide an excellent and entertaining service as well as delicious food including succulent steaks, fish and seafood as well as the delicacy *foúskes,* barnacles. The restaurant also has a small, exclusive wine cellar where wine connoisseur Stávros pours out 120 different wines by the glass. He even has bottles of the very exclusive Greek Traminer and Gewürztraminer in his cellar. *Odós Orféos 28 | tel. 22 41 02 44 69 | www.mamasofia.gr | Moderate*

LOW BUDGET

If Rhodians want to eat a good, inexpensive and authentic dinner, they like to go to *Ouzerí To Stenó (Odós Agíon Anárgyron 29 | tel. 22 41 03 59 14)* in the New Town. A carafe of Ouzo costs 7 euros while Mezédes start at 2.50 euros and a kilogram (2.2 lbs) of fresh sepia (enough for 5 people) only costs 18 euros.

Drop-down prices for delicious fish can be had at the weekly market from Aegean Fish *(Mon–Sat 11am–4pm | Odós Klavdíou Pepper 1 | on the road to Kallithéa | New Town)* **(U C1)**. Choose any fish from their market stall and they will fry or barbecue it for you at the takeaway price. The self-service buffet also offers a good selection of sides and salads for you to eat at long tables.

MANDALA (123 D5)
"Evolutionary cuisine" is the stated aim of the Greek-American chef and his team in the small terrace restaurant that has turned into the destination of choice for foreigners and artists living in the Old Town. The food, like the music, is multicultural. *Odós Sofokléous 38 | tel. 22 41 03 81 19 | Moderate*

MARCO POLO (122 C4)
Spiros and Efi, two Hellenes who love Italy, have created a small restaurant in the romantic courtyard of house in the Old Town where you definitely need to make a reservation. Choose from around ten freshly-prepared daily specials that often include a light version of moussaká made with yoghurt or a tuna steak that you can order "rare to medium" if you prefer. *Daily | Odós Agíou Fanoúriou 42 | tel. 22 41 02 55 62 | Expensive*

SOCRATOUS GARDEN (122 B3)
Enjoy a relaxing break under palm trees in this splendid garden with its own parrot in the middle of the Old Town. An ideal stopover between all the centuries, for an ice cream or drink served by a friendly, efficient staff. Not the perfect place to dine. *Odós Socratoús 124 | tel. 22 41 02 01 53 | Moderate*

INSIDER TIP **TA MARASIA** (U B6)
This rustic taverna attracts virtually no tourists. That's why the owner does everything to entice his regular customers with freshly made salads, fish and sea food. *Odós Agíou Iánnou 155 | New Town | tel. 22 41 03 07 45 | Moderate*

WALK INN (122 C5)

This modern pub-like restaurant is frequented by cosmopolitan Rhodians and foreigners living on the island all year round. The pizzas and burgers are excellent, and changing Greek specialities from the kitchen are advertised on the chalkboard. On Sunday afternoons and evenings you can sometimes listen to live music from Greek Rembetiko to Rock 'n' Roll. *Platía Doriéos 1 | tel. 22 41 07 42 93 | Budget*

SHOPPING

BLANC DU NIL (122 B1)

For fans of light, flowing fabrics, this French fashion company, also known as the all-white clothing store, has two stores in the city where you will find an array of white, 100 percent Egyptian cotton clothing for men and women. *Néa Ágora | near the bus terminal | New Town* and *Odós Pindárou/Odós Alchadef | Old Town* (123 E4)

Shop till you drop on Socrates Street followed by a well-earned drink

INSIDER TIP HARIS COTTON (123 D4)

The Athens designer team of Haris and Eva present two new collections for men and women every year made from cotton and linen. Matching accessories are also provided. *Platía Ippókratous | Old Town | www.hariscotton.gr*

KABERIS (122 C4)

Have you acquired a taste for authentic Greek coffee? You can buy a pack of freshly ground beans in this tiny coffee roastery to take back home. *Odós Sokratoús 77 | Old Town*

KAMÍROS (122 B4)

Are you looking for leather goods made directly on the island instead of imports from China? Then visit Níkos and Vassílis who make everything from belts and handbags to sandals and dog leads in their own shop; they also keep hind leather in their workshop. *Odós Sokratoús 175 | Old Town*

PLATÍA KYPROU ● (122 B1)

This tiny square abounds in boutiques selling international fashion labels such as Paul & Shark, Trussardi, Oysho, Versace, Armani, Migato, Diesel and many others. It also has the largest selection of umbrellas in Southern Europe. People always wonder why so many umbrellas are sold on an island that sees so much sunny weather. The answer lies in the past when the island was given special tax concessions and umbrellas were far cheaper here than elsewhere. You can also buy another piece of hand luggage

Tired of the city and its museums? Then breathe in the sea breeze at Elli Beach

to transport your purchases back home. *New Town*

INSIDER TIP RHODOS ART STUDIO (U B2)

A store full of individual items all at affordable prices. Jacon Hatzantonis is an avid painter and because most people have run out of room on their walls, he has branched out into painting sandals, belts, handbags and pebbles from the beach. He finds his work far more satisfying than his previous profession as a food chemist for a world famous brewery. *Odós Mandilára 20–22 | New Town*

VASSILÁRAS (122 C5)

Níkos Vassiláras was an ambassador for Greece in Brussels, designed a nuclear air-raid shelter for the president of Nigeria and made a name for himself as an acclaimed artist. He has now returned to his roots to open his own jewellers after an apprenticeship as a goldsmith. He specialises in pendants which he makes from old wristwatch mechanisms. *Odós Omiroú 42 | Old Town*

LEISURE & BEACHES

SEGWAY TOURS (123 D4)

Nothing can throw you off balance? Then jump on a Segway to explore the Old Town. These two-wheel, self-balancing scooters can guide you around the cobbled streets of the city. Escorted by a guide, you can go on a two-hour tour by day or a three-hour tour by night. *2 hours 59 euros, 3 hours. 85 euros | Odós Miltiádou 8 | Old Town | tel. 22 41 11 24 09 | www.rhodessegwaytours.com*

BEACHES

The city's beaches are not quiet, off-the-beaten track places. Stretching 4 km/2.5 miles along the coast, *Elli Beach* (U C1–2) is the closest beach to Rhodes Town located between Mandráki and the Aquarium. The nearest bar is always a stone's throw away as is the water's edge. A 3m/10ft high diving platform is just 20 m/65 ft away from the promenade. Paragliders can be spotted gliding over the bay while the sea is full of paddle boats and water-skiers. The pebbly beach between the aquarium and airport (U A–B 1–3) is an alternative on less windy days. Bathing boats leave Mandráki Harbour for the beaches along the east coast and down to Líndos while you can reach many of the island's other beaches by bus from Néa Agorá. This makes the island's capital the perfect base for your holiday.

ENTERTAINMENT

Greeks will only frequent the discos and clubs in Faliráki and other holiday resorts if they like socialising with an international crowd. The hotel quarter in the New Town between the streets 28is *Oktovríou* and *Georgíou Papanikóla* caters entirely to the whims of tourists. Greek locals prefer to hang out in the Old Town in the evenings, especially in the tiny INSIDER TIP district between the Ibrahim Pascha Mosque and Platía Ippokrátous (123 D4). After midnight, these narrow streets vibrate with sounds coming from the small bars and intimate clubs which also organise live performances. A smaller crowd also gathers at the *Platía Ariónos* in front of the former Turkish Baths.

CAFÉ CHANTANT ● (123 D4)

A truly authentic taste of Greece. Locals come to listen to the traditional sounds of Rembétika folk music which has its roots in the 1930s working class and opium caves and is today part of the counterculture in Greece. From midnight, ten musicians and singers will perform almost without any break. When a party of locals really gets going, the dancing never stops. Foreign visitors should preferably take the role of a spectator so as not to spoil their fun. Each drink costs around 10 euros, but the Greeks tend to order a bottle of whisky per table (100 euros). Minimum charge is 25 euros per person. *Sat midnight–5am | Odós Aristotélous 22 | Old Town*

CASINO ● (U B2)

Have you ever set foot in a casino? The island's gambling hall is a majestic hangout, suitable for the likes of James Bond. Built by the Italian fascists as the hotel *Grande Albergo delle Rose*, this impressive building has the air of a palace. Admission is free and you are not obliged to play. If you still dare to play and win, you can then afford one of the 33 luxury suites *(Expensive)* in the casino – with a butler thrown in. *Tables open Mon–Thu 5pm–4am, non-stop Fri noon to Mon 6am | slot machines 24 hours a day | minimum age 21 years | admission 6 euros | Odós Georgiou Papanikolaou 4 | Hotel and casino tel. 22 41 09 75 00 | www.casinorodos.gr*

COLORADO (U A2)

The place to let your hair down. Locals gather here to watch the live performances. The venue often plays Greek rock. *Daily from 10:30pm | tickets for live events approx. 10–15 euros incl. the first drink | Odós Orfanídou 57 | New Town | www.coloradoclub-rhodes.gr*

WHERE TO STAY

AVALON (122 C3)

Although you are not likely to meet the legendary King Arthur, this hotel lies next to the Avenue of Knights. All six 35 m2 large suites open up to a private veranda overlooking the tranquil courtyard where breakfast is also served. The proprietor Déspina has tastefully decorated every room individually. A caddy is also available to transport your luggage from the taxi. *6 rooms | Odós Charítos 9 | Old Town | tel. 22 41 03 14 38 | www.avalonrhodes.gr |* Expensive

INSIDER TIP **CAVA D'ORO (123 F4)**
The only hotel on the island to have private access to the city walls. Dating back 700 years, this small and relaxed guesthouse is located in the former Jewish district. Breakfast is served in the small courtyard right next to the city walls and the hotel's interior design has a certain chivalric charm. The owners care most attentively to the needs of their guests and provide good advice on what to see and do. Taxis can drive up to the entrance. *13 rooms | Odós Kistiníou 15 | tel. 22 41 03 69 80 | www.cavadoro.com |* Moderate

ERMIS (HERMES) (122 B1)
Located in close distance to most of the sights and attractions in Rhodes Town, this modern hotel named after the messenger of the gods is just one minute away from the bus terminal, excursion boats, Néa Agorá and the capital's bustling shopping street and just five minutes from the Old Town. Most rooms offer a sea view over to Turkey and the staff are extremely friendly – the breakfast buffet is for those who like biscuits and cake for breakfast. *35 rooms | Odós Nik. Plastirá 5 | New Town | tel. 22 41 02 76 77 | www.hermesrhodes.gr |* Moderate

MEDITERRANEAN (U C1)
A city break and beach holiday rolled into one. This modern, six-storey hotel is situated directly on the promenade and also has its own large outdoor pool. Open all-year round, it is just 10–15 minutes on foot to Mandráki Harbour and the Old Town. *241 rooms | Odós Kos 35–37 | New Town | tel. 22 41 02 46 61 | www.mediterranean.gr |* Expensive

OLYMPOS (122 C4)
Geórgios and María Charákis offer rooms to tourists travelling on a shoe string. Their love of bright colours and folkloric kitsch is visible everywhere but the guesthouse is authentic. *7 rooms | Odós Fanoúriou 56 | Old Town | tel. 22 41 03 35 67 | www.pension-olympos.com |* Budget

INSIDER TIP **SPIRIT OF THE KNIGHTS (U C5)**
This exclusive boutique hotel in the Old Town with only six suites and a whirlpool in the garden is managed in a very environmentally-conscious manner: it was renovated using only wood from stewarded forests, and even the radiators are made of marble instead of metal. All furnishing textiles are made of organic fibres, and the beds are suitable for allergy sufferers. Recycled paper is used, and solar power supplements the electricity from the public grid. Guests can hire bicycles free of charge. *Odós Alexandrídou 14 | Old Town | tel. 22 41 03 97 65 | www.rhodesluxuryhotel.com |* Expensive

INFORMATION

TOURISM DIRECTORATE FOR THE DODECANESE ISLANDS (122 A1)
Odós Papágou/corner of Odós Makaríou | tel. 22 41 02 32 55 | ship and bus timetables, plus opening times of museums, in front of the building

MUNICIPAL TOURIST INFORMATION OFFICE (122 B–C1)
The main office is located on *Platía Rímini (tel. 22 41 04 43 33);* other offices can be found in the Archaeological Museum and during the summer at the cruise ship terminal.

WHERE TO GO

FILÉRIMOS ★ (119 E3) (🗺 G5)
Do you have a head for heights? Then drive up the 267m/876 ft Filérimos Hill where you can spend a good hour admiring the view from its plateau at the top. You will find yourself in another world surrounded by the smells of herbs and the shrill buzzing sounds of cicadas in the pine trees and towering cypress trees. Restored by the Italians in the 1930s, the 10th century *monastery* is a truly romantic setting popular as a wedding location among Rhodes local couples. Nestled in green countryside stand the scant remains of the acropolis belonging to the ancient city of *Ialissós*, the ruins of a tiny temple dedicated to the Goddess Athena from the 3rd/2nd centuries BC. The foundations of an early Christian basilica and several chapels have also been preserved. Easily overlooked at first, the small church of *Geórgios Chostós* (Saint George) is set back into the slope. The medieval frescoes inside appear to depict kneeling knights and the eight-point cross of the Knights of St John .
Follow the alley lined with cypress trees to a viewing platform with a cross from where you are treated to the sight of planes landing and taking off at the nearby airport and a far-reaching view along Rhodes' west coast. As a souvenir buy a miniature bottle of the herbal liquor *Sette Erbe* which the Monks have been distilling here for centuries. *Excavation sites: April–Oct daily 8am–8pm, Nov–March Tue–Sun 8:30am–3pm | admission 6 euros | the other paths are freely accessible | 3 miles from Ialissós, 10.5 miles from Rhodes Town (bus connection only in the summer)*

An attraction with panoramic views: Filérimos Hill topped with a monastery

IALISSÓS (TRIÁNDA) (119 E2) *(🕮 G5)*
Three tourist resorts merged into one: With over 11,000 inhabitants, Triánda also known as Ialissós, is not only the island's second largest resort, it merges with its neighbours *Ixiá* and *Kremastí* to form the tourist centre of the west coast. A right-hand turn at the traffic lights towards the sea is only worth the journey for those with an interest for windmills and icons. Located on the road to the sea is the studio of icon painter *Vasílios Periklís Sirímis (Mon–Fri 9am–5pm | Odós Iérou Lóchou 34 | tel. 69 77 71 77 93)* who, like his father before him, has painted many of the churches on Rhodes and welcomes English-speaking tourists. There is also a beautifully renovated *windmill (daily | Budget)* on the sandy beach which today is used as a café.

IXIÁ (119 F2) *(🕮 G5)*
If high-rise buildings and gigantic concrete blocks of apartments do not appeal to you then the west coast resort of Ixiá next to Faliráki is not your kind of place. This is a popular destination for package tour holidaymakers as well as windsurfers who come to this resort close to Rhodes Town for the excellent surfing conditions (see p. 99).

KALLITHÉA THERMAL BATHS ★
(119 F3) *(🕮 H6)*
Bathe differently: No sand, no beach. This fjord-like bay with gently sloping rock banks offers an alternative destination for sunbathing and swimming with its relaxing beach bars, sun loungers beneath palm trees, pine trees and parasols. Constructed under Italian rule, the oriental-style dome of this art deco spa is an impressive sight. The crescent-shaped spa is famed for its once healing thermal waters. *May–Oct daily 8am–8pm, Nov–april daily 8am–4pm | admission 4 euros, Nov–April 2 euros, access to the beach bar free after 8pm*

KRÍTIKA (119 F2) *(🕮 H5)*
It's not worth a stop but the single-storey houses lining the coastal road from the airport to the city stand empty and beg the question what they were originally built for. A tiny mosque provides a clue: When the Turks conceded power over Crete in 1898, several hundred Muslims moved to the Ottoman-ruled Rhodes and built the town of Krítika. Their descendants later emigrated to Turkey but the houses still belong to them.

INSIDER TIP **SÍMI** (0) *(🕮 0)*
What an amazing sight! Tourists grab for their smartphones and cameras as soon

as the ship glides around the cliffs into the harbour of Sími. All three sides of the bay are covered in pastel-coloured houses spilling down the rocky coast. Overlooking the harbour is an elaborate bell tower which crowns the beauty of this idyllic village. At a time when all over Greece picturesque old buildings were torn down for the sake of "progress" to be replaced by faceless concrete blocks, the 2,600 inhabitants of the island of Sími decided instead to renovate their old houses or build new ones in keeping with tradition. The islanders are reaping the rewards of this wise move to this day: Sími rates as one of the most beautiful islands in the Aegean. In high season, there is a constant stream of boats arriving between 11am and 3pm. Sími's attractions include the large monastery at *Panormítis,* the upper part of the main village which offers a very beautiful view of the harbour and the small beach at *Pédi.*

Should you decide spontaneously to stay overnight, you need only inform the personnel on the ship and ask in one of the hotels or travel agencies at the harbour about a room. We recommend the hotel *Nireus (40 rooms | by the clock tower | tel. 22 46 07 24 00 | www.nireus-hotel.gr | Moderate)*. The food at the traditional taverna *Diethnés (tel. 22 45 07 16 74 | Budget)* near the bridge is also good. *Daily, boats from Mandráki Harbour, no need to book in advance; ferries operate several times per day.*

Soak up the breath-taking view as you glide across the Aegean to the isle of Sími

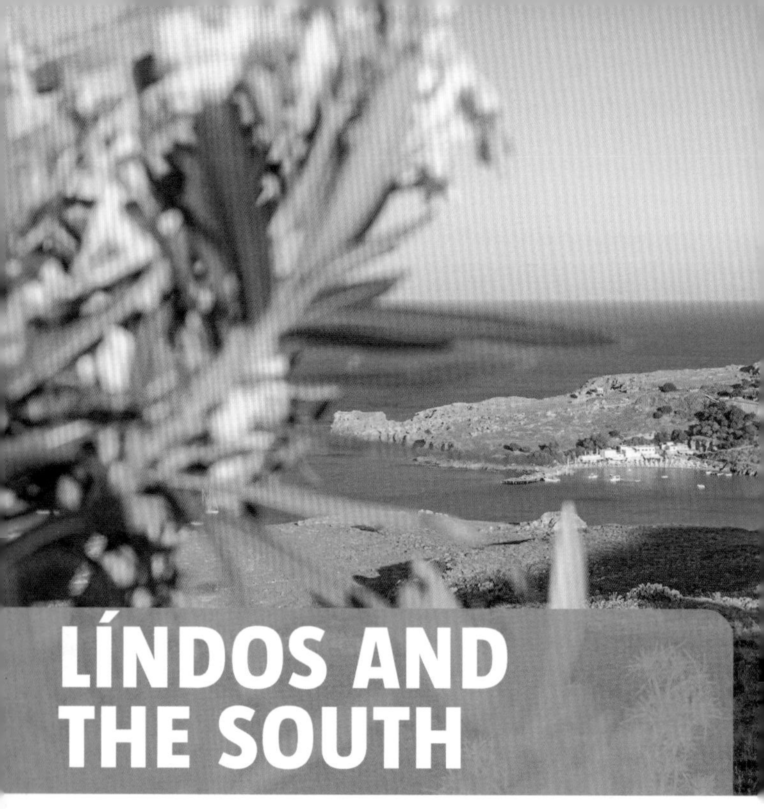

LÍNDOS AND THE SOUTH

Maybe the joy of Rhodes lies in the close juxtaposition of cultures. Everyone finds what they are looking for without searching too hard. And often discover beauty and new experiences where they least expect them.

In summer, the unbelievably beautiful village of Líndos attracts huge crowds of tourists who make their way either on foot or by donkey up to the world famous Acropolis. In contrast, very few holidaymakers set foot in most of the other mountain villages in the island's south. The modern beachside hotels in Kiotári and Plimmíri are mostly all-inclusive affairs yet villages such as Monólithos and Apolakkiá rarely attract anybody other than its own inhabitants. From the party vibes on the splendid sandy beach in Líndos, the windsurfers in Prassoníssi at the island's most southerly point to the solitary Cape Foúrni and the hippy, laid-back beach bar near Gennádi – Rhodes caters for every taste.

The landscape is equally diverse. Monólithos feels like Switzerland by the sea while the region around Kattaviá resembles the African savanna. Líndos is an archaeological treasure and the far south mainly appeals to history and art lovers with its handful of churches, monasteries and castles. Here you can ride on donkeys and horses, spot deer on the roadside and soak in the tranquillity. Even if you are based in the north, it's well worth staying at least one night in this region.

Photo: Acropolis at Líndos

Fall under the spell of the mythical landscape – relax in the quiet villages or take a dip in the pleasant waters of the east coast

APOLAKKIÁ/ MONÓLITHOS

(120 A–B2–3) (A–B 10–11) **Rhodes also offers refuge away from the masses. The neighbouring mountain villages of Apolakkiá and Monólithos are ideal for this.** You can stay in small hotels, will quickly get to know the locals and are guaranteed a peaceful night's sleep. Large, by Rhodian standards, the inland village of Apolakkiá (pop. 600), like Monólithos (pop. 330), has only been discovered as a tourist destination in the last few years. Daily life here goes on at a gentle pace as the people make a living largely from the cultivation of cereals and honeydew and water melons.

SIGHTSEEING

ÁGIOS GEÓRGIOS KÁLAMOS

St George's Chapel, entirely decorated with paintings, has no artistical value, but lies in an idyllic spot above the west coast and offers an panoramic view towards the large neighbouring island of Kárpathos – a good place for a picnic. *Freely accessible | 900 m (984 yd) off the road between Apolakkiá and Monólithos; well signposted*

Not much remains of the former castle of the Knights of St John at Monólithos

INSIDER TIP ÁGIOS GEÓRGIOS VÁRDAS

Do you "collect" churches? This tiny, single-nave church in the woods is of art-historical importance. Inside, frescos which date back, like the building itself, to the 13th century remain intact. They depict scenes from the life of Christ and also the Virgin Mary. Other figures include St George, to whom the church is dedicated. *Permanently accessible | 1300 m (1422 yd) beyond the Platía of Apolakkiá on the road to Monólithos, signposted from the opposite direction and reached via a 1.7- mile-long dirt road*

CASTLE RUINS

The knights built their castles in some truly amazing locations. In Monólithos they chose a gigantic stone finger which towers over the surrounding barren landscape. Don't worry though; the way up to the castle is harmless, involving a five-minute walk from the road up a rocky path. Only the outer walls, a whitewashed chapel dedicated to St George and a few ruined buildings have survived. The best time to enjoy the view across the sea is just before sunset. *Freely accessible during the day | on the road to Cape Foúrni | Monólithos*

FOOD & DRINK

THE OLD MONÓLITHOS ★

The food served here is something special. The proprietors, Manólis and Déspina, lived for a long time in South Africa and their travels have influenced their cooking. They use only fresh, regional ingredients and all traditional recipes have a refined touch. Their stuffed courgette flowers, which they serve between May and August, are a true delicacy as are, for the more adventurous, the snails which they collect after rainfall. *Daily | by the village church | Monólithos | tel. 22 46 06 12 76 |* Budget

WHERE TO STAY

AMALÍA

This hotel is at the heart of village life, directly on the village square. The rooms are next to and above the taverna with the same name. Everything here is basic, but the service is friendly and it's more than adequate for an overnight stay. *15 rooms | on the village square | Apolakkiá | tel. 22 44 06 13 65 |* Budget

MONÓLITHOS VILLAGE

A self-catering option in five basic yet contemporary-furnished studios (20 m²) fitted with a kitchen; a communal washing machine is also there. *On the main road | Monólithos | tel. 22 46 06 12 91 | www.thomashotel.gr |* Budget

INSIDER TIP HOTEL THOMÁS

The place for adventurous, outgoing types in search of something different. Young village locals gather here in the evenings to chill out with the hotel's young proprietor Thomás, who incidentally also owns Monólithos Village. Thomás welcomes all his overnight guests with a glass of the national distilled spirit *soúma* and preserved fruit. He can help you plan a hike or mountain bike tour or book jeep tours, wine tastings and cookery courses and can even organise stargazing from a local telescope with an expert guide. Most people who come here don't want to leave. *10 rooms |on the old village road | Monólithos | tel. 22 46 06 12 91 | www.thomashotel.gr |* Budget–Moderate

WHERE TO GO

ÉMBONAS (118 A–B5) (*🗺 C8*)

This large village (pop. 1200) on the western slopes of the Atáviros was once one of the most original and genuine on the island. Residents made a living from wine growing, animal husbandry and textile weaving. The wine growers and farmers are still here, but the original character of the place has been lost, thanks to the building of numerous (some as yet unfinished) new buildings. Émbonas is no longer a "must-see" destination. If you do come, however, visit one of the wineries along the main road – although not necessarily the ultra-modern Emery winery, which is popular with bus tour groups. Wine tasting here takes place against an industrial backdrop; in

MARCO POLO HIGHLIGHTS

★ **The Old Monólithos**
First-class taverna in Monólithos, off the beaten track
→ p. 52

★ **Acropolis of Líndos**
The postcard motif of Rhodes – with fabulous views far out to sea
→ p. 56

★ **St Mary's Church**
The church in Líndosis tells stories like a picture book → p. 58

★ **Mojito Beach Bar**
A different kind of all-inclusive place: although you pay, your day at the beach will exceed your wildest expectations
→ p. 64

the smaller establishments, things are far cosier. You can eat well at the butcher's-cum-taverna *(signposted | tel. 2246041247 | Moderate)* run by the Bákis brothers in the centre of the village. They only use meat from the region, including venison in the winter months.

INSIDER TIP CAPE FOÚRNI
(120 A2–3) *(⊞ A10)*

Experience breath-taking scenery on the zig-zag drive down to the Cape. You can clearly mark out the beaches and the Cape from above. A sign on the first of the two beaches, *Alyki Beach,* reads "Please keep it wild", a fitting description also for the beach's tiny bar. Nobody cares how you choose to bathe down here. Just before the road ends at the second beach, the 400-m (437 yd) *Foúrni Beach,* you can spot an ancient relief on a rock to the right. It shows the ferryman, Cháron, taking the souls of the dead across the Acheron river to the underworld. On the rocky peninsula beyond, there are a number of graves from Hellenic, Roman and Early Christian times; a path leads to an Early Christian cave church *(permanently accessible).* A path (easily walkable with sturdy shoes) criss-crosses the peninsula.

KATTAVIÁ (120 B5) *(⊞ B13)*

A poor, almost down-trodden village yet with an authentic charm: the platía is nothing more than a widening in the road covered in old tarmac. Around the square stand four, usually empty tavernas, the prettiest of which is the *Taverne Penelope (daily | Budget)*, resembling a village museum. The best food is cooked by Eftichía and her sons Dimítris and Manólis in *Eftichía (daily | Budget)*. The village as well as the plateau on which it stands are North African in influence. The landscape bursts with colour in spring, only to dry out in summer to resemble the African savanna. Head off the main road towards the east coast and you will see the impressive ruins of a large old silk factory standing isolated on your right-hand side. The bell tower of the *Agios Márkos* Church stands on your left towering over the old cow sheds next door: before the war Kattaviá was the centre of the island's dairy production.

INSIDER TIP MESANAGRÓS
(120 B4) *(⊞ B12)*

The clocks must have stopped here around the end of World War II. The 30 or so inhabitants of the village in the Koukoúliari hills still live in traditional one-room houses. Young people are a rare sight, most of them having moved to Rhodes Town or to one of the holiday idylls on the east coast. The el-

Kite fliers' paradise in Prassonísi in the island's south

derly remain and are delighted at anyone who has a little time to spare and sits down for a chat at the little coffee house, the INSIDER TIP *Kafeníon O Tsambíkos (Closed Mon | Budget)*. The owner worked for many years as a hotel bar tender, speaks English proficiently and has many anecdotes up his sleeve to keep guests entertained. He also has the key to open the medieval *church* opposite which was built using many architectural features of an early Christian basilica. An Antique column is used as a door lintel while colourful mosaic remains dating from 500 BC decorate the courtyard.

Some 2.1 miles to the south, on the road to Lachaniá, is the tiny *Ágios Thomás* church. His feast day is "Thomas Sunday'" the Sunday after Easter, when there is a popular, bustling parish fair under the old cypress trees in front of the church.

PRASSONÍSSI (120 B6) (*🕮 B14*)

Speed, waves and strong gusts of wind – windsurfers rave about the best surfing conditions on this sandy beach, stretching around the island's southern tip. Winds of up to 50 km/h (30 mph) are reached in high summer with waves over 2 m/8 ft high on the eastern side. Although a paradise for professionals, beginners should steer well clear. There are three surf centres based in the far south which also organise parties in summer. Non-surfers can enjoy the view out to sea, hire sun loungers and go for a swim in the designated bathing zone to the east. Two hostels and three tavernas invite guests to stay the night. Wild camping is also tolerated on the beach and sand dunes. Don't worry if you hear some shots ring out – the road from Kattaviá to Prassonísi passes through an exercise ground for tanks from the Greek army.

SIÁNA (120 B2) *(🗺 B10)*
Swarms of tourist buses stop over in Siána on their tour of the island. Reason enough to keep on driving – the village offers no attractions.

SKIÁDI MONASTERY (120 B4) *(🗺 B12)*
This inland monastery is famous as the place on earth where the icon of the *Panagía Skiadiní* (Mother of God) is kept – when she is not on tour, as she likes to travel. According to local popular belief, she performs true acts of wonders. The famous icon on the iconostasis cannot be overlooked: gilded and wrought rolled silver entirely cover the figures of the Virgin Mary and the Baby Jesus, except for their face and neck. Many votive offerings are placed near them. In the weeks leading up to Easter, the Virgin is brought for one or more days to the surrounding villages according to a strictly regulated plan where it stays in the church or the private houses of generously donating locals. This is supposed to give the entire community God's blessing. Romantic dwellers can also spend a night in one of the monastery's basic yet clean cells *(donations welcome)* in the summer. You can also just watch the sunset which is spectacular and well worth the walk up. *On the tarmac road from the west coast to Mesanagrós*

LOW BUDGET

Parking in Líndos kosts 3 euros per day (Please note: pay and display ticket machines give no change!). You can leave your car for free on the ring road or the cul-de-sac leading to St Paul's Bay. From there, a shuttle bus service *(50 cents)* operates to the village centre.

The taverna *Savvas (daily)* on the main road in Lárdos near the Platía is a rather inexpensive, but particularly good traditional-style restaurant. The *moussaká* or a pork chop only costs 60 euros.

LÍNDOS

(121 F3) *(🗺 F11)* **Líndos (pop. 800) is the most beguilingly beautiful village on the island, crowned by a radiant temple on the acropolis rocks behind the steadfast castle fortifications.**

This whitewashed village sweeps up the green hillside from the sea below, nestled between the Acropolis on one side and the tomb rocks on the other. The entire ensemble stretches between two beaches and the narrow lanes are still vibrating when the village's 80 donkeys have long since gone home for a well-earned rest.

SIGHTSEEING

ACROPOLIS OF LÍNDOS ★
By donkey or on foot? It's your choice entirely, but up you must if you want to see the most spectacular Acropolis outside of Athens. The way up is well signposted and begins right behind the ticket booth. A tiny terrace overlooking the village's golden sands is the perfect spot to catch your breath and take a photo of a relief carved into stone of an ancient war ship. The carving is a tribute by the locals to their Admiral Agesandros who

Líndos steals the show with its spectacular Acropolis

scared off pirates lurking in the waters around Rhodes at the beginning of the 2nd century BC.

A steep flight of stairs, with medieval on your right and ancient on your left, climbs up to the Acropolis from the ship's relief. You then reach the entrance gateway of the Knights of St John. The knights had little time for antiquity and believed temples to be pagan in essence. So they basically flattened the ancient relics they found here and built their own fortifications. The Danish, Italians and Greeks restored the site over the last century and reconstructed the columns to give a good impression of what the ancient Acropolis once looked like. The information boards picturing reconstruction drawings help the imagination. When you walk up the wide flight of stairs to the highest plateau, just imagine living in ancient times and making the pilgrimage to the small temple of Athena Lindia, the town's patron saint. You would only have gained a glimpse of the columns (only some of which have been reconstructed) shortly before reaching the peak because your view would have been obstructed by a colonnaded walkway or stoa, 87 m/285 ft in length and extending across the entire Acropolis. The sight must have been enough to take your breath away.

Relax and take in the view overlooking St Paul's Bay, the ancient port of Líndos. In year 51, the apostle Paul landed here when he visited Rhodes. The entire village now stretches out below you, offering the perfect aerial photo opportunity..

Luxury real estate: captain's houses in the alleys of the picturesque village

April–Oct daily 8am–7:40pm, Nov–March Tue–Sun 8:30am–2:40pm | April–Oct admission 12 euros, Nov–March 6 euros, donkey ride 6 euros one way

CAPTAIN'S HOUSES

A halfway decent house in Líndos sells for nothing less than one million euros: a fact which has seen the rich and wealthy from all over the world return to the town. These highly priced properties were originally built by Lyndian merchants and captains who sailed to all corners of the globe. The carved-relief façades and doors are evidence of their wealth and prosperity. From the inside courtyard, paved with a mosaic of black and white pebbles, you enter the living areas.

The *sála*, the largest room in the house, is always located opposite the entrance. This is where the family slept and where guests were received. The walls of the *sála* were decorated with precious, painted ceramic plates. The oldest were probably brought back by sailors as souvenirs from Turkey; later, potters from Líndos are said to have produced their own, famous "Lindian plates". As they were not meant for eating off, but as wall decorations, they have a kind of recess in the back on which the plate can be hung by a nail. Modern versions are to be had in every ceramics atelier and from souvenir shops.

Some of these old architectural gems are today rented as holiday homes (see "Where to stay"). If you're lucky, you may catch a glimpse inside one when you walk by. The only captain's house open to the public is the café *Captain's House Bar* (see "Food and Drink").

ST MARY'S CHURCH ★

As the legend goes, there was once a young devout man who was so attractive that he was persistently chased by the women. However he wanted to remain celibate so he asked God for his help. In return, God placed a dog's head on the man's head and he was then left alone. This man is known to most as Saint Christopher, the patron saint of travellers. In the St Mary's Church in Líndos (15th century), he is INSIDER TIP depicted in the bottom row of saints on the right-hand side wall. The other 80 frescoes on the walls and in the dome were painted around 1800 and also tell interesting stories. On the back wall, you can see how the righteous are led by Peter into paradise and how the sinners are transported by fire into the mouth of a monster where hell's punishment awaits them. More cheerful are the illustrations of the biblical story of Creation in the uppermost rows of images. The pictures here tell the story of how God created the world, the animals and the first man, Adam. The pictures would also have you believe that Eve was made from one of Adam's ribs – something you can discuss in your next coffee break. *Daily 9am–5pm | admission free | on the main alley*

THEATRE

On the lookout for more traces of ancient history? This open-air theatre with a former seating capacity of 2000 houses the remains of 27 rows of seats and is evidence of the prosperity of this town 2300 years ago. It lies at the foot of the Acropolis rock and provides the perfect backdrop if you are sitting at one of the cafés on the square.

FOOD & DRINK

Beauty has a price. Eating out on rooftop terraces and in the courtyards of captain's houses is a little more expensive than elsewhere on the island – but snacks and gyros are also available here at affordable prices.

INSIDER TIP ARCHONTIKO

No matter whether you order langoustine and succulent steaks or just vegetables and stuffed wine leaves – the proprietor Dímitri and son Sávvas treat all their guests the same. The atmosphere is for everyone to enjoy: tables are set on the gallery of a traditional Lyndian living area, in the courtyard or on small terraces with a fine view of the illuminated Acropolis. *Daily from 6pm | main alley Ágios Pávlos 488, upper part | tel. 22 44 03 19 92 | www.archontikolindos.com* | Expensive

CAPTAIN'S HOUSE BAR

Owner Sávvas dreams of one day leaving his business in the hands of his children and spending all his days fishing. His tiny café bar in front of the old captain's house has a laid-back atmosphere where you can sit and relax while pondering on the decorated façades and a salon with splendid wooden ceiling. Sávvas speaks excellent English and enjoys chatting with his guests when they stop

St Mary's Church is a landmark between the roofs of Líndos

off for a drink on the way down from the Acropolis. *Daily 10am–7pm | Odós Akroleos 243 | tel. 22 44 03 12 35 |* Moderate

INSIDER TIP MARIA'S

Unpretentious, affordable, well-established taverna in the upper part of the village. There may not be a fine view, but you are more than compensated by the fine Greek food on your plate. *Odós Agíou Pávlou | on the alley leading down from Yannis Bar | tel. 22 44 03 13 75 |* Moderate

MÁVRIKOS

The very first fine-dining taverna to open in Líndos is still the town's most popular address. With views of the beach, Acropolis and village, many a celebrity has dined on the restaurant's veranda. The oven-baked lamb as well as all types of fish and seafood are delicious – such as the sea urchin salad or sword fish in caper sauce. *Daily 8:30am–11:30pm | on the small roundabout at the village entrance | tel. 22 44 03 12 32 |* Expensive

NEW GATO BIANCO

Looking for the best Italian on Rhodes? Then go no further than the "new white cat" in Líndos. Finest, authentic Italian cuisine, pizza from the wood-fired oven served in a traditional setting on a rooftop terrace overlooking the Acropolis. Great hospitality and service. *Daily noon–3pm and from 6pm | on the square in front of the ancient theatre | tel. 69 34 56 22 53 |* Moderate–Expensive

YANNIS BAR

The only bar in town open all year round from morning to well into the night. Meeting point for locals and tourists alike. Its small terrace is the perfect spot to watch the comings and goings. You may see some locals working "out of office" on their laptops. Small snacks are available 24x7. *Daily 8am–3am | Odós Agíou Pávlou | tel. 22 44 03 12 45 |* Moderate

SHOPPING

BLANC DU NIL

The white clothing of this international fashion label fits nowhere better than here in the whitewashed village of Líndos. White is this town's camouflage colour. *On the main alley between the donkey "parking lot" and the church*

INSIDER TIP BLUE EYE

In vogue Greek fashion designers sell their creations here. Precarious shoes

FOR BOOKWORMS AND FILM BUFFS

The guns of Navarone – All-time classic from 1961, still rated as "one of the most exciting films ever made". It even won an Oscar for its special effects. And the storyline? David Niven, Gregory Peck, Anthony Quinn fight against the Germans and Irene Pappas plays the love interest

Reflections on a Marine Venus – The quintessential Rhodes novel (1953): Lawrence Durrell paints a vivid picture of the island before tourism arrived straight after the war

St Paul's Bay is a relaxing place to enjoy the sun, the beach and the water

and sandals by Aléxis Tsoúbos, fun summer dresses by Élena Kordáli, extravagant bikinis by Christina Kántova... Come and have fun trying on some new outfits. *On the main alley near the church*

KORI

The boutique has brought together accessories and souvenirs from Greek artists and designers "to promote the Greek spirit around the world". Take a look inside and decide for yourself if you want to support them in their mission. *Beneath St Mary's church*

VESTIUM

Casual or business fashion for young women. A mixture of young and established Greek fashion designers shares the shelves in this boutique. *Main alley, directly behind the donkey station*

LEISURE & BEACHES

Both sandy beaches on large Líndos Bay are beautiful, but pretty crowded: *Lindos Main Beach (also accessible by car)* and the smaller *Pállas Beach (only accessible on foot)*. Both offer water sports facilities. On the other side of the village, on the heart-shaped *St Paul's Bay*, there are two small pebbly, sandy beaches. Day trippers don't come here very often.

The small, modern wellness and beauty centre ● INSIDER TIP *Spa Líndos (day package 5 hours: 230 euros | on the street below St Mary's Church | tel. 22 44 03 17 77 | www.lindostreasures.com)* in an over 100-year-old house in the middle of the village is run by two Rhodian ladies who speak very good English.

ENTERTAINMENT

AMPHITHEATRE CLUB ●

First, it's starry skies, then a laser show, then the sun climbs out of the sea – clubbing à la Líndos. the large open air club stands high above Líndos Bay with a view of the town and the illluminated Acropolis. Good DJs, many live concerts in August. *July/Aug daily midnight–7am |*

on the road towards Rhodes Town, 2 km (1.2 miles) out of town | www.amphitheatrelindos.club

ARCHES NIGHTCLUBBING

Young islanders come to party under the arches of a traditional Lyndian house. The club plays funk, house, hip-hop and R 'n' B. The best parties are held on Saturdays when the local clubbers are at home. *10 m (33 ft) from the Odós Agíou Pávlou near the Yannis Bar | www.arches.gr*

LÍNDOS BY NIGHT

Classic cocktail bar in the middle of the village. Three floors, rooftop terrace. Green lights make you feel like you're in a rainforest. You can work up a sweat while dancing between the tables. *Daily 6pm–3am | on the alley that climbs up next to the donkey station | www.lindosbynight.com*

WHERE TO STAY

Air BnB, hotel booking sites and the internet have democratised Líndos. Unlike a few years ago, many holiday homes and rooms in the village can now be rented directly from the landlords themselves.

INSIDER TIP ELECTRA

The cheapest in the village: guesthouse between church and beach with seven no-frills studios for two people, slightly outdated. *On the narrow road down to Pállas Beach | tel. 22 44 03 12 66 | www.electra-studios.gr* | Budget

MÉLENOS APARTMENTS

Authentic Líndos feeling at an affordable price: The seven basic yet traditionally furnished studios open up to a sunny courtyard behind high walls and are in a central location next to the ancient theatre. The elderly landlords show genuine Greek hospitality. *Odós Emm. A. Ganotáki | tel. 22 44 03 13 32 | www.melenos-apartments.gr* | Budget

MELÉNOS LINDOS

Pure luxury and a fantastic view for 250–700 euros per suite, situated between the village and the Acropolis. This historic house is furnished with many precious items from previous centuries and has a garden to die for! The owners are well aware of their responsibility towards the environment. The hotel was largely built using local materials; all hotel textiles are made of natural fibres; you'll find organic cosmetics in the bathrooms; the waste is separated before disposal. The hotel lives by its mantra, "Luxury is not a guilty pleasure after all!". *12 rooms | Odós Akropoléos | tel. 22 44 03 22 22 | www.melenoslindos.com* | Expensive

WHERE TO GO

ASKLIPIÓ ★ (121 D3) (*D11*)

Apocalypse now! The original biblical apocalypse is on display in the 700-year old *St Mary's church* dedicated to the Feast of the Dormition of the Virgin Mary (Assumption) in Asklipió. A devout man in the 17th century painted the scene from the apocalypse inside the church. Images include the Riders of the Apocalypse and the Antichrist rising from the depths of the Earth. The other walls of the church also resemble a picture book, adorned with saints and scenes from the Old and New Testament.

Right next to the church there are two small *museums (both daily 9am–6pm | admission 1 euro)* which are both worth a visit: one is the Museum of Sacred Art, containing icons and old liturgical books – Evangeliaria – and the other is the Museum of Popular Art with an interesting collection of agricultural implements. Opposite the church and museums, you can enjoy authentic Rhodes food in the modern taverna *Nikóla (daily from 10am | Budget)* Try the sausages served with lemon instead of mustard. After a good meal, you are ready for the short climb up to the signposted castle ruins from where you are treated to splendid views of the coast and sea.

Like a biblical Graphic Novel: St Mary's Church in Asklipió

While you are visiting Asklipió, experience a unique kind of cruise by donkey. *Donkey Cruise* is organised by families from the region who rescued a group of older donkeys and gave them a new home. The stronger ones are used to carry tourists on excursions lasting one and a half to three hours through the region past old watermills and tiny chapels. Alternatively, you can just visit the donkeys to feed and stroke them. *Donkey Cruise (90-minute ride 30 euros, accompanying person 10 euros, 3 hours incl. picnic 40 and 20 euros | 200 m/656 ft off the road from Asklipió to Laérma, signposted from there | appointments: tel. 69 44 86 10 56 or tel. 69 36 55 26 54 | www.donkeycruise.com)*

GENNÁDI (121 D4) (D12)

A lively village where you can stay in small hotels and holiday homes above the coastal road yet in close proximity to the beach. A traditional place, warts and all, where messy bundles of electrical cables hang from the crumbling façades. Days are spent down on the long pebble-sand beach while the village comes alive in the evenings along its small main street where the sounds from the *Antica Café Bar* are drowned out by the bass tones from the *Southcoast Music Café* diagonally opposite. A very reasonable accommodation for all seasons is the *Summer Breeze (35 rooms | at the northern end of the vil-*

lage | tel. 22 41 04 35 43 | www.summerbreezehotel.gr | Budget). Although you don't have to stop in Gennádi if you're on a tour of the island, one place you must visit is the ★ *Mojito Beach Bar (mid May–Sept daily round the clock | tel. 69 57 67 26 82 | on Facebook | Budget)* between Gennádi and Lachaniá. A large sign and pink tractor on the coastal road point the way. Aloe vera grows by the house which proprietor Andréas and his wife Dóra use for their freshly squeezed juices and special mojitos. Brightly coloured tables and chairs stand outside between the veranda and sea on wooden platforms under the trees. Drinks and snacks are also served to the sun loungers. Guests can relax in the hammocks or even stay the night in one of the six cabanas. Live performances by a Peruvian band are held every week and some of the regular guests even bring their own instruments with them. The owner organises fishing trips with his friend a fisherman in his traditional kaíki boat; the freshly caught fish are then barbecued in the Mojito bar. If you decide not to leave, you can spend the night in one of the seven basic rooms.

GLÍSTRA BEACH (121 E3) (*🕮 E11*)

The crescent-shaped sandy beach of Kiotári is devoid of hotels and you can enjoy an unspoilt view of the bay. It has

With hotel complexes like this one, Kiotári has become an attractive destination for holidaymakers

become a popular stop among tourists travelling around the island due to its location directly below the coastal road. It is advisable to follow the crowds.

IPSENÍS (121 D3) *(🗺 E11)*
The small, white nunnery west of Lárdos is not what you'd call a major attraction in itself. It was built in the 19th century and the bell tower was added in the 1960s. What makes it worth a visit, though, is the journey to get there through olive groves and pinewoods. The nuns are hospitable, the area around the nunnery exudes a sense of peaceful tranquillity. The experience is made more memorable if you climb the gentle slope, following the pilgrim's route past the stations of the cross. *Daily 8am–12:30pm and 4pm–6:30pm*

KIOTÁRI (121 D3) *(🗺 D11)*
In summer a INSIDER TIP train passes through Kiotári which curiously transports more cuddly toys than paying guests. Not content with owning just one attraction in this all-inclusive hotel resort, the train operator has also built the village's only other sight, a large knight's castle *villa (not open to the public)* which stands on the left-hand side of the road when you leave the village in the direction of Asklipió. Since most of the hotels are all-inclusive, the resort has very few tavernas and bars. If you are not housed in one of these complexes, it's only worth stopping at the shopping centre located next to the sea along the coastal road. There you'll find the INSIDER TIP *Silver Art Works Shop Natur Arte (Mon–Sat 10am–1pm and from 5pm | www.natur-arte.com)* owned by Timo Alb, who worksa lot with operculum, the lid of a species of sea snail. Here you can also have your favourite beach pebble or seashell set in silver for an affordable price. You can watch it being made – a very personal souvenir.

LACHANIÁ (120 C5) *(🗺 C13)*
Have you ever dined with a priest before? Although the village taverna INSIDER TIP *Acropole chez Chrissis (daily | main through road | tel. 22 44 04 60 32 | Budget)* officially belongs to his wife, the priest often helps out in the restaurant, peeling potatoes, washing vegetables and is always willing to be photographed in his robes. Or you can order just a coffee here and then drive down to his village church where right next door is the modern *Plátanos (daily | tel. 22 44 04 60 27 | Moderate)* restaurant serving some of the island's best Rhodian cuisine.

A friendly greeting awaits you in the isolated Thári Monastery

LAÉRMA (121 D2) *(🕮 D10)*
This village lies almost in the centre of the island. There's nothing going on, but it's worth stopping off to visit the taverna **INSIDER TIP** *Ingo (daily from 9am / on the main road towards Thári Monastery / tel. 22 44 06 10 71 / Budget)* for a taste of excellent Rhodian cooking. It was named after a mountain. The landlord, Panayótis and his wife Stamatía will serve you excellent *pitaroúdia,* a kind of spicy veggie burger, or grilled vegetable platter.
Then head along the tarmac road to the nearby ● *Thári monastery (daily 8am–sunset / freely accessible)* hidden away from sight in the forest. Enjoy the hospitality of the monks living here and admire the well-preserved frescoes inside the ancient church which dates back to the 14th century.
Return to Láerma and follow the well-signposted path through the forest to the *Elpida Ranch* (see p. 98), a relaxing place surrounded by nature where you can try your hand at horse-riding or archery. The ranch is owned by a friendly couple who warmly welcome you into their home.

LÁRDOS (121 E3) *(🕮 E11)*
Although certainly not beautiful, Lárdos has an authentic charm. Kafenías and tavernas serving rustic food cluster around the village square in the old town on the side of the coastal road which faces away from the sea; there is also life in the village during the winter months. The new Lárdos is situated 2 km/1.2 mile away along the beach to Péfki. On the way you pass a small *local heritage museum (daily 9am–3pm | admission 3 euros)*, which shows how the inhabitants used to live in Lárdos. The friendly nuns of the *Ipsenís Nunnery (daily 8am–12:30pm and 4pm–6:30pm)* enjoy the quiet life undisturbed by the village's tourism. Dating from the 19th century, the nunnery can be reached by following a 5 km/3 miles long road inland from Lárdos. It's worth the drive to soak up the peace and tranquillity of the landscape around which can be best enjoyed by following the pilgrim's trail with crossroad stations up the gentle hillside.

PÉFKI (121 E3) *(🕮 F11)*
Péfki is the perfect beach holiday destination. Indeed the only attraction is its long sandy beach which is divided into small coves by rocks. There is no old village or even any sights; the resort is solely geared to the needs of summer holidaymakers with all the usual water sport stations along the coast as well as small hotels, restaurants, cafés and bars along the main road. You can walk to Líndos in 90 minutes or explore the island's south by scooter or car.
The best restaurant to enjoy dinner is the *Ártemis Garden (daily from 11am | on the main through road | tel. 22 44 04 83 65 | Moderate)*, where you can also get excellent pizza. At *Tsambíkos (daily from 11am | below the road to Líndos | tel. 22 44 04 82 40 | Budget)*, vegetarians will also enjoy themselves. The great food is only topped by a far-reaching view over the town and the sea from the large roof terrace. Later in the evening, *Péfkos by Night* is the popular venue in the village centre playing hits from the sixties to the latest mainstream pop on its veranda.

PLIMMÍRI (120 C5) *(🕮 C13)*
Up until 2015, Plimmíri was a tiny hamlet home to a harbour, a handful of fish tavernas and a few houses nestled in the surrounding fields. This all changed however with the opening of an enormous hotel complex called *Tui Magic Life* in the middle of nowhere. The region has attracted no new businesses or tavernas because the entire hotel village is all-inclusive. Its long pebbly beach can accommodate many sunbathers and the *fish taverna (daily | Moderate–Expensive)* continues to serve authentic, rustic food. The ruins of a monastery (founded in 1837) stand immediately behind the taverna. Many elements of an early Christian basilica were incorporated into its well-preserved *church:* Plimmíri was a small town 1500 years ago. Mussel collecting is still a popular pastime on the beach and *glass bottom boat* rides to Prassoníssi are a new attraction. Boats stop off at the desolate *Paradise Beach* and at a wreck of a traditional kaíki boat.

VLÍCHA BAY (121 F2) *(🕮 F10)*
Several large hotel complexes are located along the wide 1 km/0.6 mile long pebbly beach at Vlícha Bay. Most of the hotels deceivingly incorporate the word Líndos into their names yet you can't even see Líndos from this bay – and there is no path leading to the idyllic town 3 km/1.8 mile away.

THE CENTRE

Rhodes is chameleon in character, changing its appearance constantly as you drive across the island's centre. The juxtapositions are clearly visible yet you should also look out for the finer nuances.

The fertility-bringing, hilltop chapel of Tsambíka and the hotel high-rise blocks in Faliráki stand worlds apart. And while the Eucalyptus Alley of Kolímbia is testimony to meticulous planning, the maze of old streets in Archángelos and the new face of Afántou show a more chaotic side to the island. Everywhere is welcoming yet each offers a unique experience. The completely unspoilt Tsambíka Beach is almost like a mini Sahara desert by the sea. Standing on the Profítis Ilías not only feels like being in a forest, you can even stay the night in a chalet-like historic hotel. A visit to the verdant Butterfly Valley can be combined with a short horse ride through a vineyard and an ostrich omelette in the nearby ostrich farm. You can also explore the inside of a sycamore tree near Archípolis.

History has left behind a wealth of sights and attractions in this region. A stroll through the ancient town of Kámiros takes you virtually as far back in time as archaeological evidence can take you. You can also play knights in several castles and be witness to a sad family drama in a tiny Byzantine church. And there is enough to fill your appetite from the freshly caught fish served at the taverna in Kámiros Skála to the island's pizza capital, Afántou.

 Photo: Kámiros

Heady disco nights, a mountain, antiquity and the beach: Rhodes' centre has something for everyone

AFÁNTOU

(119 E4) (*G7*) **Afántou is not pretty yet many of its guests come back year after year.**

They crowd the pavements and the maze of one-way streets which are virtually devoid of parking spaces, undisturbed by the architectural mayhem surrounding them and the fact that there are no views of the sea from Afántou. They take pleasure in the town's bustling authenticity, know the locals and even have Greek friends. After a day spent on the long stretch of sandy beach, the locals (many of which speak a foreign language) and tourists all come together in the town's many tavernas and coffee houses.

FOOD & DRINK

FOUR SEASONS

This stylishly modern bar serves ample portions of pizza and pasta and the mixed grill is bombastic. Regular guests order the *kléftiko,* succulent lamb cooked with potatoes and vegetables, which comes fresh from the oven at 6pm every day. *Daily from noon | on the road from the platía to the southern end of the village | tel. 22 41 05 19 90 |* Budget

SERGIO'S
Fancy a pizza? Then try the best on the island here. You can even order takeaway pizza to be delivered to your own apartment. *Daily from 1pm | 20 m (66 ft) from the main square | tel. 22 41 05 20 50 |* Budget

Sunbathing away from the masses is still possible at the beach of Afántou

O THIÓRIS
Looking for a snack to satisfy your hunger? Then head to this traditional white and blue painted taverna where the Greek proprietor Theó will inform you what the kitchen has on offer today. Do as the locals do and order a little of everything. Sit in summer under the shady trees and in winter next to the open fireplace. *Daily from 8pm | Odós El. Venizélou | near the Family supermarket | tel. 22 41 05 33 40 |* Budget

LEISURE & SPORTS

The pebbly *Afántou Beach* is 40 m (130 ft) wide and 4 km (2.5 miles) long. It offers no shade at all, but there's still a lot of room since loungers, hotels and tavernas are not yet packed tight. In high season, there are a few water sports possibilities. The island's only golf course, the *Afandou Golf Course (April–Oct 35 euros, Nov–March 20 euros | www.afandougolfcourse.com)* is located between the Rhodes–Líndos road and the beach. Once an hour in the daytime, a *miniature train* on wheels (*ride: 5 euros*) plies the route from the village square to the beach.

WHERE TO STAY

AFÁNDOU SKY

Great for bargain hunters: The small, friendly two-storey hotel, built in 1991, has a lovely pool terrace and sits about 1 km (0.6 miles) from the beach. The local Platía is only 200 m (219 yds) away. *34 rooms | Odós Profíti Ilía | tel. 22 41 05 23 47 | www.afandousky.com | Budget*

OÁSIS

The proprietor Chrístos Gambroúdis has indeed created his own small oasis with bungalows and a low-rise building with individual rooms in splendid gardens. Trees overlook the pool and the delightful wooden playground appeals to both children and adults. The platía is 15 minutes away on foot and the beach just 800 m/0.4 mile. The hotel has a family-friendly atmosphere and you can also book all-inclusive..*37 rooms | on the coast road, set back a little | tel. 22 41 05 17 71 | www.oasis-hotel.gr | Budget*

WHERE TO GO

KATHOLIKÍ AFÁNTOU (119 F4) (*G7*)

Building work on the small church continued on and off for many centuries. It is worth a visit, above all for the frescos – even if art historians do not consider them to be particularly special. To reach the church, you have to drive past the village, coming from the direction of Rhodes Town. Shortly after the signpost which reads "Afántou Golf" there is a sign for Afántou Beach. Turn off here. The church is situated on the left.

PETALOÚDES (BUTTERFLY VALLEY) ★

(119 D3) (*F6*)

A good choice! Between June and August, hundreds of thousands of butterflies (in Greek *petaloúdes*) populate the 3 miles of this lush, green valley. Usually they sit with their wings closed, quite inconspicuous, on the leaves of the sweet gum tree; at other times they fill the air – and sometimes the kitchen of the taverna – in dense swarms! The insect in question is in fact a moth with black front wings and glowing orange back wings, *Panaxia quadripunctaria* – or Jersey Tiger, to give it its English name.

The beautiful countryside is worth a visit at any time of the year. It has a small *Natural History Museum (only May–Oct | visit included in the admission to the valley)* with a butterfly collection and an idyllic *taverna (Budget)*. The INSIDER TIP spaghetti served up by proprietor Theófilos, who has run the taverna with his wife and his son Dímitri since

MARCO POLO HIGHLIGHTS

★ Petaloúdes (Butterfly Valley)
At its most beautiful in the mating season of the butterflies in July/August, but always a green oasis → p. 71

★ Kámiros
A great trio: ancient town, good beach and tasty food → p. 78

★ Profítis Ilías
Have you come to the wrong place? Coffee and cakes up in the clouds, architecture and forest just like in the Alps → p. 83

1948, are top class, as is the *moussaká,* prepared fresh every day. *Mid-June–mid-Sept daily 9am–6pm, otherwise until sunset | admission mid-June–mid-Sept 5 euros, May–mid-June and mid-Sept–Oct 3 euros, Nov–March free admission, but only open sporadically*

Petaloúdes, marriage market for butterflies – can they have butterflies in the stomach?

PSÍNTHOS

(119 D4) *(M F7)*

Psínthos is the place to go for a rural dinner. For the Rhodians, the inland village surrounded by green is a historical location. It was here that the Italians defeated the Turks in 1912 and brought the island under their control. It took another 30 years for the island to become Greek. On the edge of the village, you can dine year-round in pleasant, rustic surroundings at the INSIDER TIP *Artemída House (Tel. 2241050003 | Budget)* on the road to Archípolis. The stuffed kid from the region, roasted in the oven for twelve hours, is delicious, and the miniature pancakes with various fillings, made by the proprietor's wife as a free dessert, are to die for! Salads and vegetables are from the owners' own garden or from friends who farm in the village.

INSIDER TIP VINEYARD TRIANTÁFILLOU

● (119 D3) *(M F7)*

Anastasiá Triantáfillou, daughter of the vinicultural dynasty, Emery, is a passionate wine grower. Her son Jason even studied viticulture for three years in Bordeaux. Anastasía is almost always to be encountered in this winery established in 1995 on the main road along the west coast to Butterfly Valley; she lets her customers taste the wines, sells homemade wines and the distilled spirit *soúma,* olive oils and marinated olives as well as a wide selection of natural Greek products including soap made from donkey's milk, mastic gum oil or black volcanic ash. Her son Jason takes more time out of his schedule, inviting guests to join him on the winery *(entrance/driveway is 100 m/330 ft before the ostrich farm).* The view over the vines stretches to the Profítis Ilías Mountain. Visitors are welcome to taste all wines served with accompanying snacks while the wine producer is keen to talk about his ambitious aims for the vineyard, in French or English. If you have enough time, Jason will take you on a short horseback ride around the vineyards. It is advisable to reserve in advance by phone (bookings are also taken at short notice). The owners like to take their time to show visitors around the site. *Open during the day | tel. 69 73 42 37 68 | jason.zafeirakopoulos@gmail.com | taverna: Budget*

ARCHÁNGELOS

(119 E6) (F–G 8–9) **Archángelos (pop. 5500) is a good example of how tourism does not have to be synonymous with the disappearance of everything which is fundamental to the charm of a place.**

It shares this aspect with Afántou yet the historic centre of Archángelos is far more appealing. There are old, whitewashed houses and unevenly paved alleyways. The people always seem to have more time to spare than visitors from the hectic world around them and especially from other parts of Europe. Old traditions still mean something in the "village of the Archangel" – especially on Good Friday and Saturday as well as on Carnival Sunday. The next beach is around 2 miles away below the town at Stegná.

SIGHTSEEING

CHURCH

Like a bejewelled, snow-white finger, the bell tower of the church of the Archangel Michael dominates the similarly white houses of the old part of Archángelos. The structure, with its delicate air, is a remnant of the Italian occupation. The church itself dates back to the mid-19th century. The most interesting feature is the typically Rhodian mosaic in the inner courtyard made of black and white pebbles.

KNIGHTS' FORTRESS

On a hill on the edge of the village stand the ruins of a castle built by the Knights of St John, commissioned by Grand Master Orsini in the middle of the 15th century. Close to the entrance, several coats of arms are to be seen carved into the walls, including the Orsini crest and the number 1467, the year the castle was completed. From the castle, you have a fine view over the white silhouette of the historical part of the village. It is also well suited to a picnic.

FOOD & DRINK

INSIDER TIP AFÉNTIKA

This small, unspectacular taverna, in which elderly local residents often get together in the evenings to watch television, serves up a particularly good Greek salad. Made according to the traditional recipe, twigs and leaves from the caper bush, marinated in vinegar, are also added. The proprietor is extremely friendly and often lets you have an ouzo or soúma on the house – and consequently has built up quite a following among Archángelos' holiday guests! Dishes which are not actually on the menu can be prepared specially, if ordered in advance. *In the centre, tucked away behind the Legend Bar on the road to the Post Office | tel. 22 44 02 36 40 |* Budget

HELLAS

The owner Stélios grew up in Germany, so his restaurant has some German touches, despite its very Greek name. He makes special dishes for his regulars and his daughter Stamatía loves the meatballs filled with feta cheese the best. *Daily | on the side of the town hall | tel. 22 44 02 27 06 |* Budget

SHOPPING

Traditionally, Archángelos is seen as the island's pottery village. There are a number of ceramics workshops on the main road between Rhodes Town and Líndos.

LOW BUDGET

Cheaper under your own steam: A day trip from Rhodes to Hálki. At least twice a week, you can make a round trip to the island by catamaran. Travel time: 85 minutes; stopover on Hálkí: approx. 7 hours; return ticket: 32 euros. More information: the travel agencies in the Néa Agorá in Rhodes Town or *www.12ne.gr*

Modern rooms directly at the fishing harbour of Kámiros Skála can be booked through the taverna *Aitheméni (tel. 22 46 03 13 03)* all year round for at most 35 euros.

WHERE TO STAY

DELFÍNI BEACH

For a friendly stay: This small hotel with modern furnishings is located directly on the coastal road. The umbrellas and sun loungers at the beach are free for guests. All the balconies offer views of the sea. The hotel also has a very good taverna serving fish and a trendy-styled bar. *15 rooms | Stegná | tel. 22 44 02 33 23 | www.stegna-delfini.gr |* Moderate

PORTO ANGELI

Looking for a club holiday? The complex near the beach offers plenty of sports and entertainments for visitors. Great for kids. It's best to book a package. *171 rooms | 4 km (2.5 miles) outside the village on the beach at Stegná | tel. 22 44 02 40 00 | www.portoangeli.com |* Expensive

WHERE TO GO

CHARÁKI (119 D–E6) *(F9)*

Until a few years ago, only a handful of summer houses stood on the pebble beach here. Many of them belonged to farmers from the villages of Malónas and Mássari further inland where people still live from the cultivation of oranges and mandarins. Meanwhile, Charáki has become a popular bathing resort, but does without huge hotel blocks. Visitors stay mostly in small guesthouses and holiday apartments. A pedestrianised beach promenade, with cafés, restaurants and bars, adds to the flair of the village. The apartments INSIDER TIP *Haraki Mare (10 apartments | tel. 22 41 07 45 24 | www.harakimare.gr |* Budget*)* at the northern end of the promenade are a quiet place to stay for up to five people per apartment. Take a look at the small *Ágii Apóstoli Chapel* on the village square

The breathtaking but also imposing view of the Féraklos fortress

which was decorated inside in 1997 and 1998 in the traditional style by the monks of the autonomous republic of Mount Athos.

FÉRAKLOS FORTRESS
(119 D–E6) (*🕮 F9*)

On a hill to the north of Charáki lie the ruins of the fortress of the Knights of St John, Féraklos, illuminated in the evening. It is assumed that a castle stood here in the days of antiquity. What is certain is that there was a Byzantine fortress on the site which was captured by the Knights of St John in 1306. In 1470, Grand Master Orsini had it renovated. The fortress was used above all as a prison for the prisoners of war taken by the Order and as a place of exile for knights who were guilty of misconduct. From the north side, there is a beautiful view across the fertile land around Malónas and Mássari and over the bay and sandy beach at the base of the hill. Above the bay, a touching gem is to be found, hewn into the rock face: the tiny chapel *Ágia Agáthi.* It is said to have been constructed in the 12th or 13th century. Agáthi Bay, which lies around 30 minutes walk from Charáki, boasts a pretty, sandy beach. Its 200 metres are usually rather quiet, though three beach bars have set out their tables in the sand. The fortress can easiest be reached from the beach access road, but sturdy shoes are recommended.

STEGNÁ (119 E6) (*🕮 G9*)

The remote beach village can be reached via a winding road which leads through the old, almost completely abandoned potters' village of *Petróna*. In the taverna **INSIDER TIP** *Petroná (daily | tel. 22 44 02 27 97 | Budget)*, located a little way off the road to Stegná, the proprietors Jánnis and Kiriakoúla dish up rural specialities including roast kid from their own herd, prepared in the wood-burning

The bays around Faliráki are great places to go fishing

stove and served with chickpeas, as well as many other rural specialities. The little sandy beach at Stegná is perhaps not as beautiful as the one at Tsambíka, but the bay is greener and the food at the shady tavernas is down-to-earth good-quality Greek fare. In the seafood taverna INSIDER TIP *En Plo (daily / tel. 22 44 02 25 37 / Moderate)* on the coastal road you can even order "Germans". Called *Germaní* in Greek, these brown rabbitfish got their name during the Second World War thanks to their spikes and camouflage colour.

FALIRÁKI

(119 F3) *(H6)* **Faliráki is a bustling hive of activity between June and September. The wide, sandy beach stretches 4 km/2 miles and the island's capital is just ten minutes away by bus – no wonder that the town attracts so many tourists.**
Travel operators have no difficulty finding accommodation for tourists in Faliráki; the town is full to bursting with large hotels. Most of the major multi-storey complexes line the northern end of the beach while the resort's south is the island's entertainment capital with no end of pubs, sport bars and discos and a few striptease clubs interspersed with stores appropriately entitled "alcohol world" as well as pharmacies open 24x7. The tiny harbour in the south hints at the former simplicity of this old fishing village where authentic Greek tavernas can still be found. If you continue along this road, you will come to the island's only official nudist beach and a café for stargazers. The resort offers a diverse mixture of attractions to suit most tastes: you are free to decide what you want to do and what you prefer to avoid.

FOOD & DRINK

INSIDER TIP AKTÍ
Mama Paraskeví and her son Nektários remain completely unfazed by the hustle and bustle of the tourist masses. They

run their small taverna at the harbour entrance in the traditional Greek manner – with warmth and dedication – and prefer to serve up no-frills, honest-to-goodness fare. *Tel. 22 41 08 66 32 | Budget*

INSIDER TIP STÁMA

The proprietors of this small taverna have their own fishing boat and offer their catch exclusively here. The sardine-sized *gópes* are usually always on the menu – a delicious freshly fried treat for simple tastes. The fine Greek salad is accompanied by the leaves and twigs of the caper bush – including thorns – marinated in vinegar. Believe it or not, these are not only edible, they are in fact extremely tasty. *At the fishing harbour | tel. 22 44 08 64 95 | Moderate*

STÉFANOS

Among the beach tavernas in front of the giantic hotels of Faliráki, this one is the best. It is still run by a local family and Élena is in charge of the kitchen. The menu includes a large variety of dishes as well as regional specialities. *Odós Apollónos | next to Hotel Apollo Blu | tel. 22 41 08 53 45 | Moderate*

SHOPPING

There are a host of small supermarkets and souvenir shops, but you should not expect more.

LEISURE & BEACHES

At more than 4 km (2.5 miles) long and up to 50 m (164 ft) wide, Faliráki's main beach extends from the big hotels in the north of the village to the small harbour close to the centre. Either side of this, there are a number of other beaches and rocky coves which you can reach quickly on foot or by bicycle. If you are not bothered by a rocky coastline with stones beneath your feet underwater, or if you have packed water shoes, you can walk about 700–1300m (765–1421 yds) from the northern edge of Faliráki, away from the road leading to the thermae of Kallithéa, to get to the lovely INSIDER TIP *bays of Nicólas Beach, Tássos Beach, Oásis Beach and Jordan Beach.* Each beach has a small beach bar and sun loungers along the flat rock plateaus and stony pools. There is even an INSIDER TIP official nudist beach at the southern end of the bay where umbrellas and sun loungers can be hired. Water sports of all kinds are on offer on the main beach, in front of the big hotels. Motor boats with up to 30 HP are available to hire even to those who don't have a sailing license.

ENTERTAINMENT

BED

Number one with the British tourists, this mega-disco is equipped with the most powerful sound system on the island. Laser shows, foam and paint partys lure the party crowd. *Faliraki Shopping Centre | Odós Kolokotróni 37*

BEDROCK INN

Wasn't Bedrock the name of the town where Wilma and Fred Flintstone once lived? Yes but this club is not your average Stone Age dwelling, attracting a young crowd of partygoers. The club specialises in themed nights, ranging from beachwear to toga parties. *Leofóros Pigón Kallithéas 68*

LIQUID

Clubbers are explicitly invited to dance on top of the bars in this club. Those who prefer to keep their feet firmly on the ground have two dance floors to choose from, playing house and electronic downstairs and R'n'B and hip-hop upstairs. You can chill out on the sofas in the VIP area. *Odós Afrodítis 1 | northern street parallel to Bar Street*

WHERE TO STAY

INSIDER TIP AQUARIUS

Looking for an all-out beach holiday and exciting nightlife but in more intimate accommodation? Then this small beachside hotel is the right choice for you. Five, ground-floor rooms are just a stone's throw from the sea while the other rooms nestle around the pool. The sun loungers on the beach and around the pool are free of charge and the beach bar is open all day and night in the main summer months. *27 rooms | 100 m (328 ft) north of the harbour | tel. 69 32 41 35 58 | www.aquarius-faliraki.gr | Moderate*

ÉSPEROS VILLAGE

One of the most beautiful hotels on the island. Like a village in its own right, it is situated on a slope high above the hustle and bustle below. Free shuttle bus to the beach. *195 rooms | tel. 22 41 08 60 46 | www.esperia-hotels.gr | Expensive*

WHERE TO GO

ANTHONY QUINN BAY
(119 F4) *(H7)*

This small, rocky cove near Ladikó got its name because the Greek military junta presented it as a gift to the famous actor – in recognition of the fact that it was here in 1961 that he shot the film *The Guns of Navarone* and therefore introduced the island to millions of moviegoers all over the world. The democratically elected government later reclaimed the land, and it is now accessible to all. *On the coast road in the direction of Líndos, turn left after 1000 m (0.6 mile) towards Ladikó; diagonally opposite the Hotel Ladikó, a dirt road leads to the bay*

INSIDER TIP KOSKINOÚ (119 F3) *(H6)*

An authentic Greek village, even near Faliráki. The taxi ride to Koskinoú costs just 6 euros and is worth the trip for its maze of narrow lanes with small houses and old mansions. A 20-minute round-trip walk through the village begins at the church and leads past the local museum in a typical old residence as well as the good taverna *O Giánnis (tel. 22 41 06 35 47 | Budget)*. Head left from the restaurant and then go left again to get back to the village square beneath the church.

LADIKÓ (119 F4) *(H7)*

Guests in search of peace and quiet are well served here. There are two hotels, two bathing bays with tavernas, otherwise there's nothing far and wide. Stay in pleasant surroundings at the *Hotel Ladikó (42 rooms | tel. 22 41 08 55 36 | www.ladiko-hotel.gr | Moderate)* with its small garden, only 150 m (492 ft) from the sandy beach.

KÁMIROS

(118 B4) *(D2)* **Sunbathing and sightseeing – you can get the best of both worlds in ★ Kámiros.**

First visit the excavations in an ancient town, followed by the beach and the waterfront tavernas. You can spend a whole day in the town, easily reached by bus.

SIGHTSEEING

EXCAVATIONS

Fed up of temples and ancient Gods? Here you can find out how the normal folk lived 2100 years ago. Kámiros was the smallest of the first three Rhodian cities and had its heyday in the 6th century

BC. The town was built on a slope, and the view from the houses spans green fields, pinewoods and olive groves. Inhabitants of the ☀ upper part of town could even see the coast. You can still enjoy the same view today because no hotel or industrial plant stands in the way at the moment. The residents, however, paid dearly for their town's exquisitely beautiful location. In 226 BC, an earthquake destroyed almost every building, but the town was re-built. Around three centuries later, in AD 142, another major quake razed Kámiros to the ground. This time no one wanted to stay, and Kámiros was abandoned.

The ruins of "Rhodian Pompeii" date largely from the 3rd and 2nd century BC. The lower terrace of this hillside site was hewn into the rock, supported by mounds of earth and a retaining wall and enlarged to form the agorá, or market place. To each side, there once stood shrines, statues and residential buildings. The small temple in the centre was probably dedicated to Apollo.

To the east of this, there is a festival ground with low tiers of seats for spectators. This was probably the venue for rituals in honour of the god. To the west, the arena borders a residential area which lies directly on the ancient main thoroughfare. This leads past a public baths and a fountain house (in many places, ceramic pipes hark back to the ancient water supply and drainage system) and further residential areas as far as the Acropolis. Only a few traces of its once magnificent buildings remain. *Approx. Easter–Oct daily 8am–7:45pm, Nov–easter Tue–Sun 8:30am–2:30pm | admission 6 euros, Nov–Easter 4 euros*

FOOD & DRINK

INSIDER TIP OLD KÁMIROS

Located opposite the side road leading to the excavations and directly in front of

Never ceasing to impress: the breath-taking view from Kámiros to the sea beyond

the bus stop, the more traditional of the two beach-front tavernas is simply furnished yet boasts an extremely friendly service. Langoustines and other shellfish are kept in the large basin and feel free to haggle prices with the owner. *Daily | tel. 6945411730 | Moderate*

INSIDER TIP PORTO ANTICO

Its modern counterpart next door has a more beach bar feel partly beneath the trees' shades – the food in both tavernas is equally good. *Tel. 2246041241 | Expensive*

BEACHES

The beach in front of both tavernas is the nicest and widest in the resort. Both tavernas serve drinks and food to customers on the free beach sun loungers.

WHERE TO GO

HÁLKI (118 A–B 1–2) *(M A–B 1–2)*

The tiny island of Chálki is worth the short boat ride. Only 500 people now live there, but the main village of Nimborió is really cute. Even as you enter the harbour, you notice the old houses painted in pastel colours. More and more of them are gradually being renovated and rented out in summer as holiday homes, chiefly to British visitors: *Halki Direct (tel. 2246045005 | www.halkidirect.com)*. The local minibus or the island's taxi will shuttle you to the three beaches, to the deserted village of *Chorió* with Crusaders' castle and to the monastery *Ágios Ioánnis* in the island's far west. This region shows how rugged and barren the landscape can be on the Greek Aegean islands.

The fastest and easiest way to get to Hálki is to take the *Catamaran (www.12ne.gr)*, which runs several times a week

A Mediterranean dream: Nimborió, the capital of the island of Hálki

from Rhodes Town. You can also book day-long tours. A charter boat runs from Hálki to Kámiros Skála daily at 6am and returns to the island around 2:30pm. During the summer season, excursion boats run daily between these two locations. One option for staying the night is the guesthouse *Kleánthi (7 rooms | tel. 22 41 05 73 34 | Budget)*.

KÁMIROS SKÁLA (118 A4) (*B8*)
A few isolated houses, an occasional passenger ferry and a handful of fishing boats at the quay in front of the low-lying rocks. The boats sail over from the small islands off the coast of Rhodes, bringing their catches ashore. Refrigerated trucks then transport the fish to the island's hotels and tavernas. Locals gather on the large veranda of the taverna *Altheméni (daily | tel. 22 46 03 13 03 | Budget–Moderate)*, to eat fish and succulent pork chops served with Greek salad and marinated capers. With plenty of room between the tables and Greek music playing in the background, the taverna has hardly changed since 1957 when the grandfather fed the entire family with his tiny fishing boat which still stands prettily decorated on the veranda.

KASTRO KRITÍNIAS
(118 A5) (*B–C8*)
Dating back to the time of the Crusaders, this small castle holds a solitary position overlooking the vast Aegean Sea. The castle is open to the public and is just a two minutes' walk from the car park. You can also spend a leisurely hour on the small shady veranda of the no-name *taverna (Budget)* beneath the car park. The owner only serves homemade, traditional Greek food. *Kritinía*

KOLÍMBIA

(119 E5) (*G8*) **A 2 km/1.2 mile long road lined with eucalyptus trees leads you into the town of Kolímbia. With over 40 hotels – most of which are all-inclusive – the resort competes with Faliráki and Ixiá yet it has its own distinctive charm.**

Most of the hotels are pleasantly spacious, low-rise complexes set at a good distance apart. The town only has a few (yet long) streets all named after European capitals and you will find no loud clubs or bars anywhere. The beach is not one long stretch of sand; it divides into two more intimate coves.

FOOD & DRINK

TO NISÁKI
The name translates into "small island" and this taverna is dedicated to fish through and through. Most of what the

proprietor puts on the tables comes from the Aegean. Next door, he also runs a bar, and the whole set-up is just a few steps from the beach. *At the northern edge of town | tel. 22 41 05 63 60 | Expensive*

WHERE TO STAY

KOLYMBIA SUN

This welcoming, informal hotel with swimming pool is around 200 m (219 yds) from the beach: an all-inclusive complex which also offers rooms big enough for three adults and a child. *65 rooms | tel. 22 41 05 62 13 | www.kolymbia.gr | Moderate*

WHERE TO GO

INSIDER TIP ÁGIOS NIKÓLAOS FOUNTOÚKLI (118 C5) (*🕮 E7–8*)

No house to be seen far and wide, just low-lying rocks and green countryside. A 600-year old church stands on the road side where goats and sheep sometimes congregate in front around the fountain and fruit producers sell their goods: a splendid spot for a small picnic. Founded by a high-ranking Byzantine official on Rhodes, the church was also the setting for a family tragedy. The official and his wife are depicted on a fresco next to the west entrance. On the opposite wall, the couple's three children are represented. An inscription relates that they all died at around the same time, probably as a result of some kind of epidemic.

ARCHÍPOLIS (119 D5) (*🕮 F8*)

A different kind of treehouse: In the ancient INSIDER TIP *sycamore tree* in front of the stairs to the *Ágios Nektários* monastery near the inland village Archípolos, an entire family can fit inside its completely hollowed-out trunk.

EPTÁ PIGÉS (119 E5) (*🕮 G8*)

It is always pleasantly cool under the huge sycamore trees in the valley of the "Seven Springs". The many peacocks seem to like that, too. The feature which attracts visitors to this popular destination is a 186-m(203 yds)-long underground water channel dug during the Italian occupation of the island. At the end of the tunnel is a pond amidst a gently rolling, lush green landscape. Walk over the hill above the tunnel to get to this idyllic spot. A word of warning: since the whole area is a protected source of drinking water, you will have to do without taking a dip in the pond. Directly behind the car park, you'll find the taverna *Seven Springs (daily | tel. 22 41 05 62 59 | Budget)*, where you can order simple Greek dishes such as *soufláki* (meat grilled on a skewer) or *paidákia* (lamb chops).

The Káto Tsambíka Monastery: home of the miracle-working icon

PROFÍTIS ILÍAS ★ (118 B5) (*D8*)

Are temperatures getting too hot? Then ride up to the island's third highest mountain. At a height of almost 800 m/2624 ft, it is pleasant up here even in summer; islanders come with their children into the forest mainly at the weekends. The Italians built a hotel up here in 1929 in the style of an Alpine chalet. Here you can get a cool, quiet night's sleep, enjoy a romantic meal or take off on a tour of the surrounding forests with the free mountain bikes available to guests. The hotel is called *Élafos (23 rooms | tel. 22 41 04 48 08 | www.elafoshotel.gr | Moderate)*.

TSAMBÍKA (119 E5) (*G8*)

If you meet somewhere in the world a man named Tsambíko or a woman named Tsambíka, you will know where they come from: Rhodes. And you will also know who was responsible for their conception. The tiny whitewashed monastery church is a place of pilgrimage to this day and is visited in particular by young women in the hope of children. While most tourists drive up half the way, female pilgrims walk (or crawl) up to pray for fertility and the chance of a child. It is said that the pilgrimage will be most fruitful if the pilgrim shoulders a sack containing a heavy stone. A path leads through a white gateway into the monastery courtyard. Women enter their name and their wish in the thick guest book lying open in the chamber on the right. On the left-hand side there is an empty chamber which serves pilgrims as a dormitory. Tsambíka's miracleworking icon of the Virgin Mary is only visible in the church on November 7th/8th. For security reasons, she stands for the rest of the year in the modern monastery *Káto Tsambíka,* located on the main road to Líndos, just 1 km/0.6 mile away from the road up to the hilltop chapel.

DISCOVERY TOURS

1 RHODES AT A GLANCE

START: ① Rhodes Town END: ① Rhodes Town	13 hours Driving time (without stops) 4.5 hours
Distance: approx. 240 km/149 miles	

COSTS: entrance fees approx. 24 euros per person
WHAT TO PACK: swimming kit, sunscreen, flat shoes with non-slip soles for the visit to the castle and the excavations, I.D. for discounts (senior citizens/students)

IMPORTANT TIPS: pick up the keys for your rental car on the evening before around 9pm if the rental agency does not open until after 8am, and return them at 9pm the following day.
Some renters allow you to return the car the next morning before they open at no extra charge.

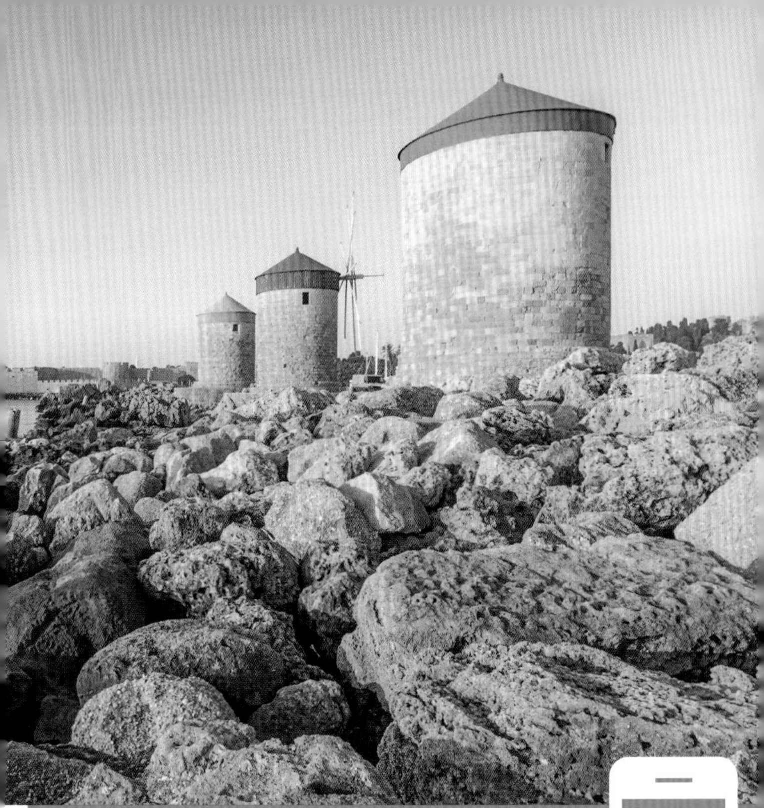

Would you like to explore the places that are unique to this island? Then the Discovery Tours are just the thing for you – they include terrific tips for stops worth making, breathtaking places to visit, selected restaurants and fun activities. It's even easier with the Touring App: download the tour with map and route to your smartphone using the QR Code on pages 2/3 or from the website address in the footer below – and you'll never get lost again even when you're offline.

TOURING APP

→ p. 2/3

This route takes you in an anticlockwise direction around the island. The advantage is that you can still get to Líndos in daylight even if you only want to hire a car for one day. Experience all the natural beauty of Rhodes and see the most important archaeological sites, romantic churches, a small fishing harbour and isolated villages. You'll still have time for a dip in the sea if you get on the road early enough.

08:00am Depart from ① Rhodes Town → p. 32 in the morning and head towards the airport. From the centre of Ialissós (Triánda) → p. 48, follow the signs up to

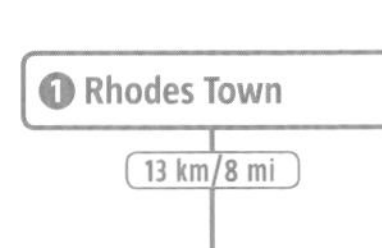

Photo: Windmills at Mandráki Harbour

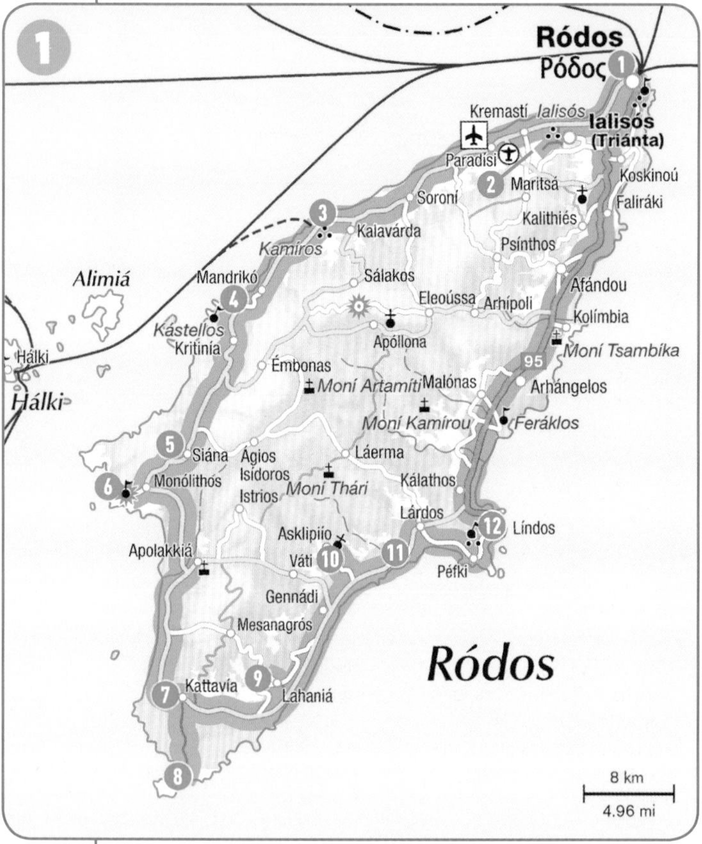

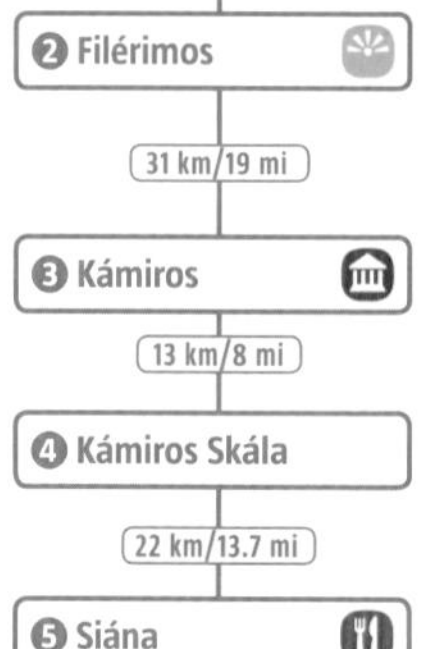

❷ Filérimos

31 km/19 mi

❸ Kámiros

13 km/8 mi

❹ Kámiros Skála

22 km/13.7 mi

❺ Siána

❷ Filérimos → **p. 47**. The open view of the coast and the island's mountains to the southwest gives you a real feel for the beauty of the Rhodian landscape.

Head back to the coastal road and follow it until you reach the excavations of the ancient city of ❸ Kámiros → **p. 78**. A good place to take a break afterwards is the fishing harbour **❹ Kámiros Skála** → **p. 81**, an ideal spot to watch the local fishermen at work.

12:00pm **Afterwards, travel up to the large mountain village of** **❺ Siána** → **p. 56**, where you can stop for a good lunch. Then work off all the calories that you have eaten

by driving just a bit further and climbing up to the 6 **castle ruins of Monólithos → p. 52**. From here you can look out over the sea to the neighbouring island of Kárpathos.

Continue along the open and still mostly natural beaches where the winds are sometimes quite strong **to the southernmost point on the island** near 7 **Kattaviá → p. 54**. After a coffee break on the village square, drive over **the well-paved road through the isolated countryside to the island's southern cape** where you will find the surfers' beach 8 **Prassoníssi → p. 55**, which resembles the Sahara in miniature.

First head back to Kattaviá and from there, continue on towards 9 Lachaniá → p. 65. For an authentic culinary experience with a rustic feel, stop in at the taverna **Plátanos**.

Follow further along the coast towards Kiotári → p. 65, where a small cul-de-sac leads up to 10 Asklipió → p. 62. The frescos on the walls of the **church** in this small mountain village are some of the island's most beautiful. **Almost right next door on the coastal road 11 Glístra Beach → p. 64**, one of the prettiest on the island, will lure you into the water for a swim.

Shortly before Lárdos → p. 67, turn to the right to head towards Péfki → p. 67 and keep driving through this coastal town to get to 12 Líndos → p. 56. As you approach this picturesque village from above, you can see its old captain's houses and countless souvenir shops as well as St Paul's Bay and the broad main beach below. The ancient Acropolis lies before you at about eye-level. You'll now realise why it is worth spending another entire day here.

09:00pm The road between Líndos and the island's capital makes for an easy and quick drive back to 1 **Rhodes Town** where you will arrive around 9pm if you choose to return on the same day. If you do not have to turn in your rental car until the next morning, you should definitely drive on to the large village of Archángelos → p. 73, where you can INSIDER TIP dine among the locals in one of the country-style tavernas in the centre of town before you make your way back to Rhodes Town.

THE OLD TOWN IN DEPTH – A DAY IN THE CAPITAL

START: ❶ Néa Agorá
END: ❶ Néa Agorá

8–12 hours
Walking time (without stops) 1.5 hours

Distance: approx. 5 km/3.1 miles

COSTS: entrance fees approx. 17 euros/person, spa pedicure 7 euros
WHAT TO PACK: IDs for elderly and student discounts

IMPORTANT TIPS: wear flat shoes with non-slip soles!

Most holidaymakers reside outside the capital. You too? Then this extensive tour of the town hitting all the sites while still offering plently of opportunities to stop for a bite to eat or do some shopping is just the right thing for you.

10:00am All bus routes from the holiday resorts into town end at the ❶ **Néa Agorá** → p. 38. First off, **stroll through the inner courtyard** with its many barbecue stands and a handful of jeweller's and souvenir shops and make your way to the two kiosks opposite, which boast the largest selection of international newspapers and magazines on the island. **Pass between the kiosks to come out on the harbour side of the Néa Agorá**, which is home to some tempting pastry shops. If you can resist the delicious cakes and ice cream sundaes on offer, **cross the street** and sit down on one of the many benches to take in the colourful array of excursion boats and sailing yachts before you. Then **wander past the restored windmills on the eastern pier to the medieval fortress tower** ❷ **Ágios Nikólaos**. This is the best place to take a photo of the Old Town centre across Mandráki Harbour → p. 36. You can also get a good snapshot of most of the huge cruiseliners docked in the neighbouring Emborikó harbour.

Once you are back at the mill pier, **follow the traffic over the short bridge into the Old Town**. Behind the parked cars, it is easy to overlook the remains of an ancient ❸ **Aphrodite Temple**. Art lovers should head to the right and explore the **Art Gallery** of the ❹ **Museum of Modern Greek Art** → p. 38. Go a few steps further and you will find yourself on the **Platía Argirokástrou**. Alongside the small pyramids of stone canonballs, this square is home to the first hospital of the Order of the Knights. **Walk straight on for another 50 m (55 yards)** until you reach the ❺ **Museum of Archaeology** → p. 34, which was the second, much larger hospital run by the Knights of St John. Even if you are not really into art, you should still definitely take a look. The two-storey arcades of the inner courtyard provide a great photo opportunity, and the large hospital ward of the Order of St John is like no other in the world.

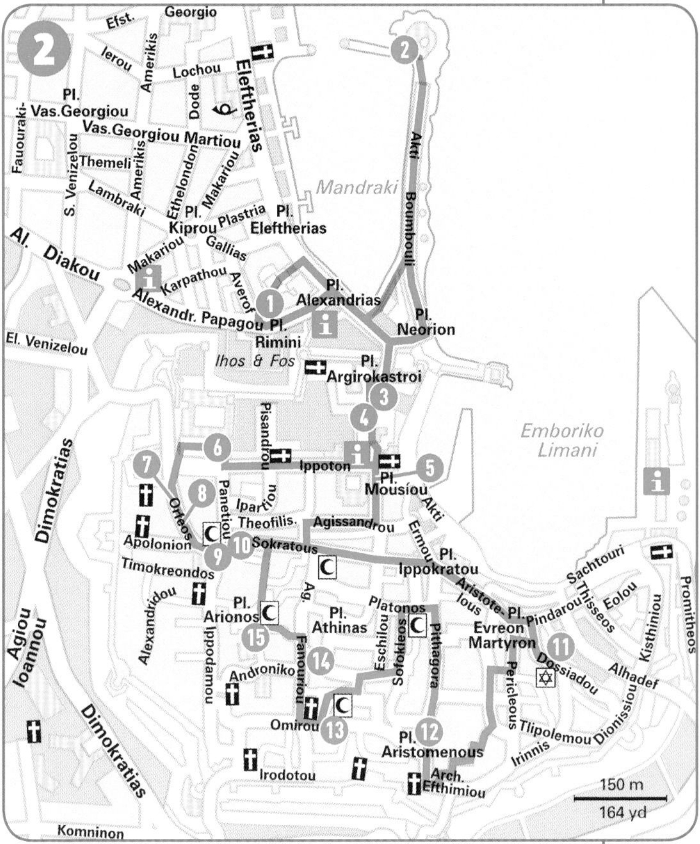

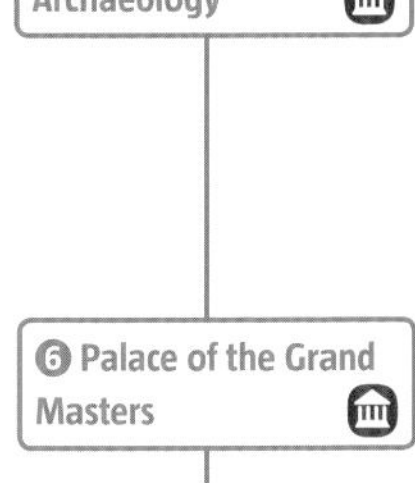

Climb gently over the pebbled cobblestones of the Avenue of the Knights → p. 39 past the 600-year-old inns of the Crusaders to the magnificent ❻ **Palace of the Grand**

❺ Museum of Archaeology

❻ Palace of the Grand Masters

It is not a television tower, but rather the Süleyman Mosque

Masters → p. 35. After inspecting the palace, it is time to treat your feet to something special. **Head right out of the Palace of the Great Masters and then go left on Odós Orféos.** Give your feet a special treat in ⑦ INSIDER TIP Magía Fish Spa *(Odós Orféos 24)*, courtesy of the small fish in the glass tubs who like to nibble away at your toes. After that, head up to the top of the ⑧ **Clock Tower** → p. 41 to get a good overview of the entire town. The entrance fee includes a refreshing drink.

01:30pm **The** ⑨ **Süleyman Mosque** → p. 38 with its towering minaret marks the beginning of the most dangerous part of the tour, at least for your bank account. **Head down** ⑩ **Odós Sokratous** → p. 38, where you can shop at your leisure and then shop some more. Shops selling jewellery, leather goods and souvenirs line Socrates Street on both sides. The best places to check out for a midday snack are the totally secluded garden café **Socratous Garden** → p. 42 at the top end and **Café Kárpathos** in the middle where you can sit under shady trees and watch as people from around the world pass by.

⑦ Magía Fish Spa

⑧ Clock Tower

⑨ Süleyman Mosque

⑩ Odós Sokratous

⑪ Kahal Shalom Synagogue

⑫ Windmill

Socrates Street ends at **Platía Ippókratou** with its expensive cafés. Go past the many souvenir shops along the street until you come **to Platía Evréon Márytron** in the former Jewish Quarter of the Old Town. **Odós Dossiádou** is home to the fully restored ⑪ **Kahal Shalom Synagogue** → p. 40. From here, the route **continues through the narrow and winding streets of the town centre**. The rump of an old ⑫ **Windmill** on **Odós Pythágora** offers a great vantage point from which to gaze over the rooftops of the Old Town and cast your eyes across the sea towards Asia Minor.

At the end of Odós Pythágora, in the area around the Ibrahim Pascha Mosque, you will find the hippest quarter of the Old Town. It might be a little sleepy in the afternoon, but in the evening, it really comes to life. **Follow along**

Odós Sofokléous to get to the Platía Doriéos where the attractive ⑬ **Redjeb Pasha Mosque** and two pleasant cafés await. **Continue along to the Byzantine church ⑭ Ágios Fanoúrios** → p. 33. After taking a look inside, head past the **Sultan Mustafa Mosque to what were once the ⑮ Turkish Baths**.

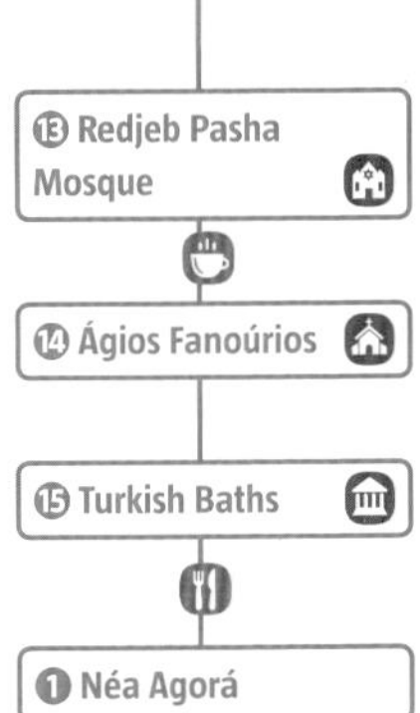

06:00pm Afterwards, you can take another stroll **through the area around Socrates Street**. Spend the rest of the evening in one of the characteristic and enjoyable Old Town tavernas before returning to ① **Néa Agorá** to catch your bus or a taxi back to your hotel.

3 UP AND DOWN THE MOUNTAINS

START: ① Faliráki END: ① Faliráki	10 hours Driving time (without stops) 4 hours
Distance: 107 km/65 miles	

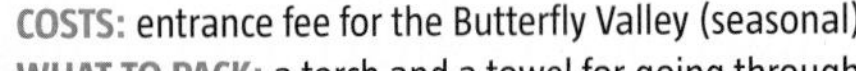

COSTS: entrance fee for the Butterfly Valley (seasonal)
WHAT TO PACK: a torch and a towel for going through the tunnels and provisions for a picnic

IMPORTANT TIP: many of the butterflies in Petaloúdes can only be seen from June to August.

This route takes you away from the coast and into the heart of Rhodes with its small villages, quaint coffee houses and authentic tavernas. It meanders up and down, often passing through pretty forests, vineyards or olive plantations. Byzantine churches and a relaxing coffee break are on the day's agenda. But, above all, you can enjoy the fantastic views of the hills and mountains across to the sea.

09:00am From ① **Faliráki** → p. 76, **drive towards the airport. Just past the western end of the airport grounds, signs clearly point the way to a side road that branches off from the main road and leads towards the Butterfly Valley in Petaloúdes.** Especially if you have kids on board, you should take a short detour to the ② **Rhodes Ostrich Farm** → p. 103 that lies along the way. Park your car at the lower (first) entrance to the ③ **Butterfly Valley Petaloúdes** → p. 71 and walk upstream and back down again.

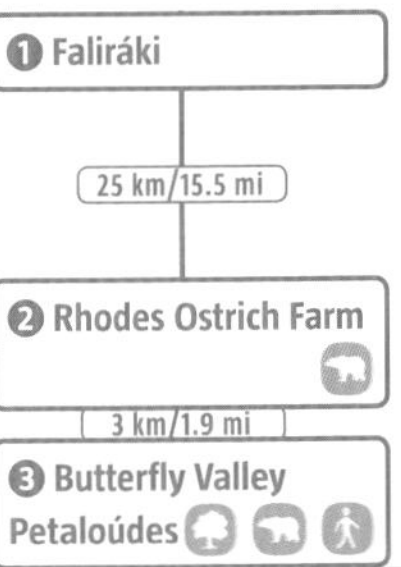

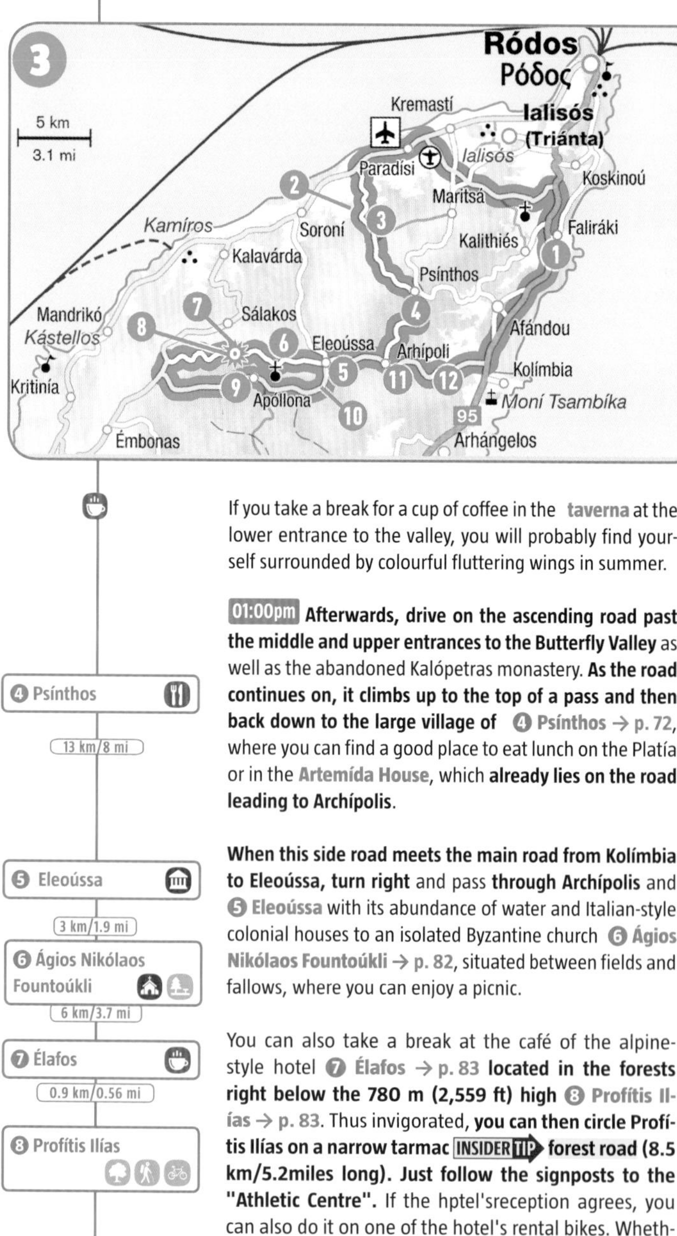

If you take a break for a cup of coffee in the **taverna** at the lower entrance to the valley, you will probably find yourself surrounded by colourful fluttering wings in summer.

01:00pm **Afterwards, drive on the ascending road past the middle and upper entrances to the Butterfly Valley** as well as the abandoned Kalópetras monastery. **As the road continues on, it climbs up to the top of a pass and then back down to the large village of** **4 Psínthos** → p. 72, where you can find a good place to eat lunch on the Platía or in the **Artemída House**, which **already lies on the road leading to Archípolis**.

When this side road meets the main road from Kolímbia to Eleoússa, turn right and pass **through Archípolis** and **5 Eleoússa** with its abundance of water and Italian-style colonial houses to an isolated Byzantine church **6 Ágios Nikólaos Fountoúkli** → p. 82, situated between fields and fallows, where you can enjoy a picnic.

You can also take a break at the café of the alpine-style hotel **7 Élafos** → p. 83 **located in the forests right below the 780 m (2,559 ft) high** **8 Profítis Ilías** → p. 83. Thus invigorated, **you can then circle Profítis Ilías on a narrow tarmac** INSIDER TIP **forest road (8.5 km/5.2miles long). Just follow the signposts to the "Athletic Centre".** If the hptel'sreception agrees, you can also do it on one of the hotel's rental bikes. Wheth-

4 Psínthos

13 km/8 mi

5 Eleoússa

3 km/1.9 mi

6 Ágios Nikólaos Fountoúkli

6 km/3.7 mi

7 Élafos

0.9 km/0.56 mi

8 Profítis Ilías

er by car, on a bike or even on foot: you will experience a mostly unknown Rhodes!

After you've returned to the Hotel Élafos, drive to the peaceful mountain villages of ⑨ **Apóllona** and ⑩ **Plataniá**. **You will then find yourself back in Eléoussa before you again pass through** ⑫ **Archípolis** → p. 82. **Just after you leave the village, look to the right** and you will see a hollowed-out **sycamore tree** below the large pilgrimage church **Ágios Nektários** with its decorative frescos.

Drive through the valley of the streambed of Loutan towards the coast and then follow the signs to turn towards the forest taverna at ⑫ **Eptá Pigés** → p. 82. Peacocks will come out to greet you before you explore the dark tunnel for a bit of an adventure.

07:00pm **At Kolímbia, get back on the eastern coastal road** and it is just another 10 km (6.2 miles) back to ① **Faliráki**.

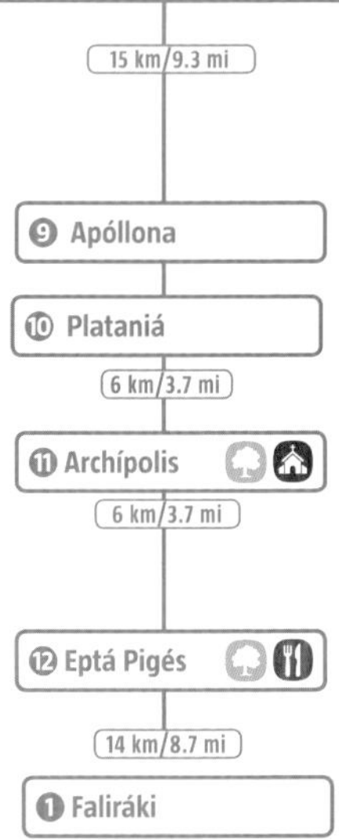

4 CYCLING THROUGH QUIET VILLAGES

START: ① Kiotári
END: ① Kiotári

Distance: 54 km/34 miles
difficult — Height: 500m (1,640 ft)

12 hours
Driving time (without stops) 4.5–7 hours

COSTS: mountainbike rental approx. 12 euros/day
WHAT TO PACK: water, a picnic, sun protection, helmet

IMPORTANT TIPS: mountain bike rental in Kiotári: **Dimitris Manias Rent a Motorbike** *(Kiotari Shopping Centre on the main street) | tel. 22 44 04 70 20 | tel. 69 77 66 57 45)* – You should definitely reserve your bikes in advance!

Pure nature: On this round-trip tour through the south of Rhodes you can explore the most peaceful side of the island along mostly wellpaved roads with little traffic. The route has many ascents in the middle, but refreshments and snacks are available in every village. This route lets you enjoy the island's natural beauty, but it also brings you closer to its people. When you stop in Kafenia, you will more than likely fall into conversation with the village's few local residents – even if facial expressions and gestures are the only common language.

❶ Kiotári

4 km/2.5 mi

❷ Gennádi

7 km/4.34 mi

❸ Vatí

8 km/5 mi

❹ Agía Iríni

2 km/1.2 mi

❺ Taverna Vrisi

0.5 km/0.31 mi

❻ Arnithá

12 km/7.5 mi

❼ Mesanagrós

2 km/1.2 mi

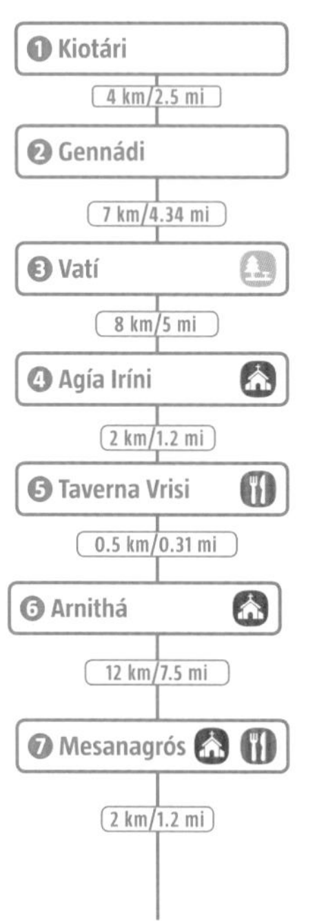

09:00am From ❶ **Kiotári** → p. 65 where you will start your trip in the morning, you should follow **along the coast until you reach the northern edge of ❷ Gennádi** → p. 63, a village that has retained its truly authentic character. **From here, the road towards Vatí, which is 7 km/4.3 miles away, forks off from the road circling the island** and leads into the middle of the island along a mostly flat stretch. **You should definitely bike into ❸** INSIDER TIP **Vatí** itself because the **village square** is well worth a stop. **Afterwards, continue upwards** through the hilly countryside full of fruit trees to the small church of ❹ **Agía Iríni** and then pass by ❺ **Taverna Vrisi** *(Daily | Budget)* with its simple, good country-style food. **Cycle on through ❻ Arnithá** with its abundance of flowers, the 19th-century **Church of St George** and an old drinking fountain.

03:00pm The most difficult stretch of the route lies ahead, but it also offers the best views. **The often dusty field track winds over the 500 m (1640 ft) high Koukoúliari hills and after 12 km (7.5 miles), you will come to ❼ Mesanagrós** → p. 54 with its ancient **village church** and the cosy taverna **Kafeníon O Tsambíkos** → p. 55. After a long, incredibly relaxing break among the rather old villagers, head back around 3pm along the last, mostly downhill stretch. If you

You're not in a hurry! Lachaniá's village square is ideal for a break

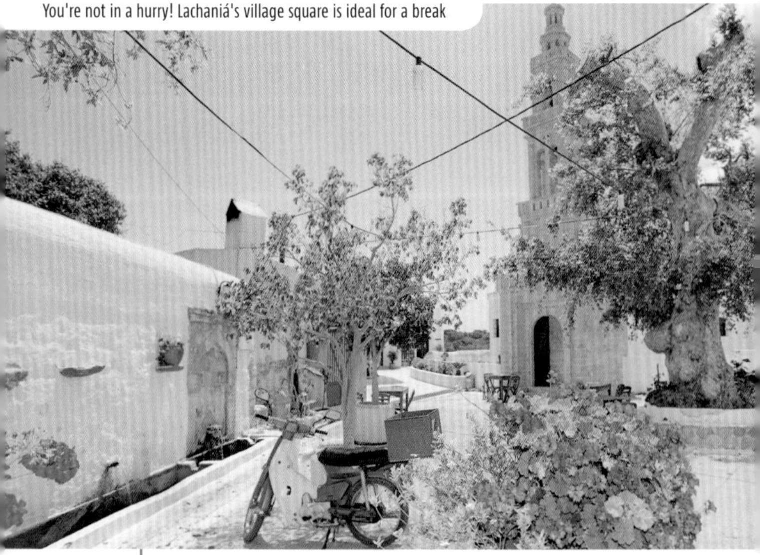

would prefer to have a picnic, the small pilgrimage church 8 **Ágios Thomás** → p. 55 in the forest directly below the road to Lachaniá is the ideal place.

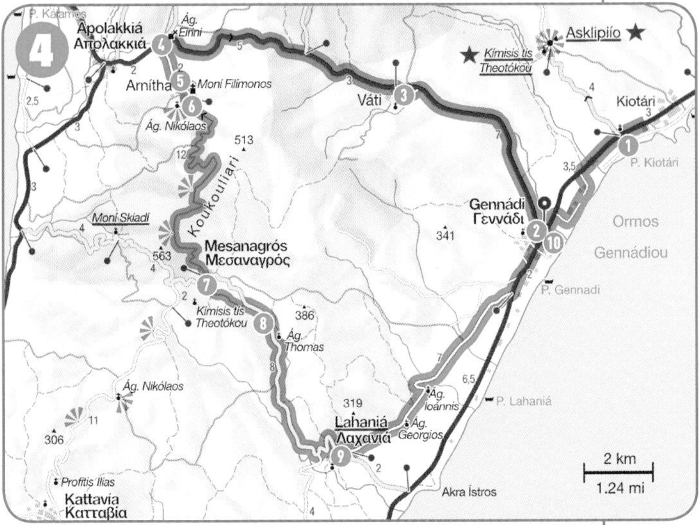

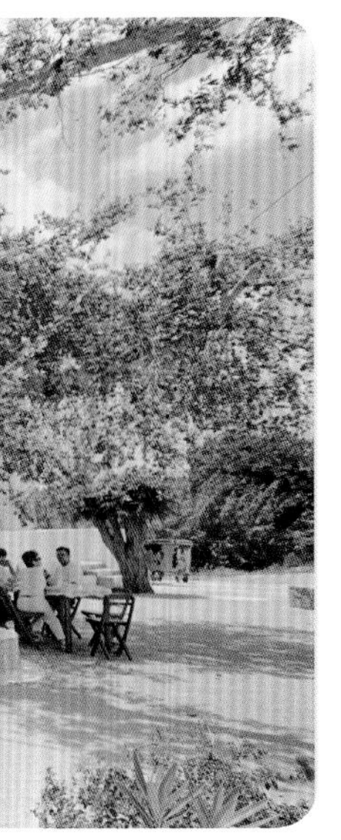

On the way to the village of 9 Lachaniá → p. 65 you will have to manage just one more short ascent. Right afterwards, you can stop in at **Acropole chez Chrissis** → p. 65, the coffee house of the village priest, or treat yourself to some of the organic fruits and vegetables. The priest is more than willing to pose for a photo in his traditional robes.

06:00pm **After Lachaniá, a long and straight dirt road forks off from the coastal road and brings you back to 10 Gennádi in 9.5 km (5.9 miles).** Here you can take a swim before you tackle the last **4 km (2.5 miles)** to 1 **Kiotári**.

8 Ágios Thomás

6 km/3.7 mi

9 Lachaniá

14 km/8.7 mi

10 Gennádi

7 km/4.3 mi

1 Kiotári

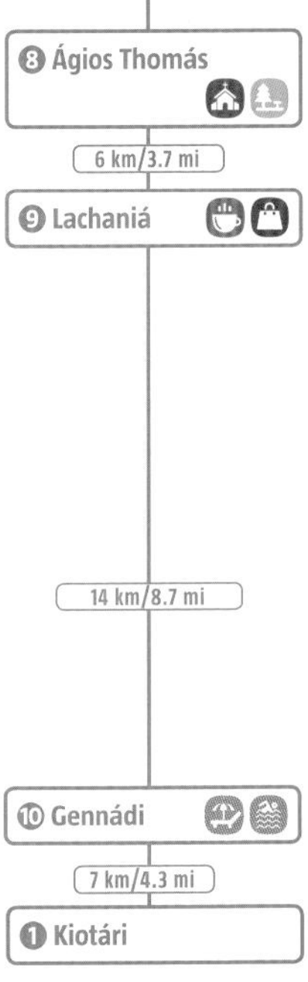

SPORTS & ACTIVITIES

On the search for the ultimate experience? Try riding on horseback through the Rhodian "prairie" or gliding along Tsambíka Beach in a paramotor.

More suited to water? Rhodes is not just a sunny but a windy island too. It offers perfect conditions for both surfers and kiters. You can also try driving a motorboat as you do not need to have a sailing license. The waters around the island are not only home to fish but shipwrecks too, making them ideal for divers to explore. Mountain bikers and hikers are also treated to unspoilt, off-the-beaten tracks inland; some of the island's rocks are even suitable for rock climbing. And what about wellness? Spa facilities are available at the large hotels as well as at an old captain's house in Líndos.

ACTIVITY HOLIDAYS

If you love a rush of adrenalin and exciting thrills, contact *Rhodos Activities Booking (tel. 69 45 99 51 68 | www.rhodesactivitiesbooking.gr)* who will help you organise a tour to suit your tastes. The Rhodian internet agency is run by two young men who offer a list of activities provided by various operators on the island. They can help you book tours and even organise transfers to and from the locations. The activities available range from riding and diving, hiking and cycling, rock climbing and windsurfing (both in conjunction with yoga), stand-up paddling, paintballing and paramotor flights. It's definitely worth checking out the website of Jórgos and Stéfanos..

Whether you want to relax or stay active on the water or on land, the best addresses for your holiday are listed below

BOAT HIRE

Pedalos can be hired on many beaches *(approx. 10 euros/hr)*. On the beach at Stegná and at Faliráki harbour you can hire motor boats ● without having to have a licence *(from approx. 37 euros/hour)*.

DIVING

Scuba diving is permitted on Rhodes at several marked stretches along the coast when accompanied by a licenced instructor. The dive center run by young Greeks, *Lepia Dive Center (Tel. 6937417970 | www.lepiadive.com)* in Péfki and Plimmíri also accommodates handicapped divers. Several boats leave daily for dive tours from Mandráki harbour in Rhodes Town. Even completely inexperienced divers can **INSIDER TIP** take their first dip down to a depth of 5–6m (16–19ft). Local providers include *Waterhoppers (Odós Kritiká 45 | Rhodes Old Town | tel. 2241038146 | www.waterhoppers.com);*

Dive Med Centre (at the Magic Life Club | Plimmíri | tel. 69 46 25 94 09 | www.divemed.gr) specialises in diving excursions in the island's south and also offers snorkelling trips departing from Plimmíri harbour.

HIKING

Rhodes is ideal walking country. However, there are no proper walking maps and no signposted trails; hiking guidebooks date quickly. If you want to see the island on foot, you are advised to book a complete hiking holiday at your local travel agency. Guided daytrips can be booked with *Impress Holidays (Odós Prágas 11 | Kolímbia| tel. 22 41 06 03 72 | www.impressnet.gr)*.

HORSERIDING

A dream destination for horse lovers: the INSIDER TIP *Elpida Ranch (tel. 69 48 13 29 77 | www.elpidaranch.eu)*: A German-Rhodian couple has created a small paradise in total reclusion between Laérma and the Thári monastery. They also have pigs and chicken, an improvised pool, a communication-friendly sun terrace and a small archery facility. children can ride on ponies, more experienced riders can even go on hacks that take several days. Everything is very laid-back; it's best to call ahead and talk about the programme that suits you best. Rather more conventional and touristy, the *Fívos Horse Riding Club (signposted on the main road | Faliráki | tel. 69 38 61 82 52 | www.fivos-horse-riding.com)* near Faliráki offers, among other things, 90-minute guided hacks along the beach, even for absolute beginners.

MOUNTAINBIKING

For mountain bikers, Rhodes provides ideal terrain. There are plenty of quiet, asphalted roads in the centre of the island and countless more dirt tracks. A particularly good agency that also offers guided tours is *Rodos Cycling (Pl. Rápti 1 | at the Hotel Sunshine Rhodes | Ixiá | tel. 69 47 30 99 11 | www.rodoscycling.com)*. *SD Bikes (Odós Kordigtónos 69 | tel. 22 41 07 35 11 | www.sdbikes.gr)* and *Rhodos Bicycle Rental (Odós Th. Sofoúli 97 | tel. 22 41 02 12 64 | www.rhodosbicyclerental.gr)* are situated in Rhodes New Town. On the west coast, *Impress Holidays (Odós Prágas 11 | Kolímbia | tel. 22 41 06 03 72 | www.impressnet.gr)* offers guided tours and rental bikes. An international bike rental agency is *www.bimbimbikes.com*. Rental bikes are brought directly to hotels all over the island and to the airport at a price. The average cost is approx. 15 euros a day and 90 euros a week.

WATER SPORTS

A variety of water sports are on offer on almost all beaches adjoining the larger hotels. You can go windsurfing, parasailing, waterskiing or sea canoeing or you can hire a pedalo.

Stand up paddling is the specialty of *Paddle Paradise (90 minute course 35 euros, 3 to 4 hour guided tour 59 euros | in front of the Limnióni taverna | Stegná Beach | tel. 22 41 03 88 93 | www.paddleparadise.gr)*. An ideal spot for experienced windsurfers is the beach at Prassoníssi in the far south of the island. Wind and kite surfers like the beaches between Ixiá and Theológos on the west coast the best. There are some busy kite stations in Fánes *(www.kite-rhodos.com, www.meltemi-kiteclub.com)*. The well protected bay at Líndos is particularly

Both in and on the water – there are lots of activities to entertain guests on Stegná beach

suited to waterskiing. A good water sports station is the *Kiotari Watersports Centre (surfing course: 10 hrs. approx. 180 euros | on the beach in front of the hotels Rodos Maris and Rodos Princess | Kiotári | tel. 22 44 02 32 79 | www.wassersport-rhodos.de).* Here, too, you can go surfing or get your catamaran sailing licence *(6–8 hrs. incl. exam fees: 280 euros)* or windsurfing licence from the International School Association for Water Sports (VDWS). In the north of the island is *Windsurfers' World (Tel. 22 41 02 49 95 | www.windsurfersworld.gr)* in Ixiá, a good address which also runs a **INSIDER TIP** *Kite Pro Center* in Kremastí *(www.kiteprocenter.gr).* Prices and sports on offer are similar to Kiotári Watersports Centre.

WELLNESS

Rhodes does not have the necessary temples for an extended spa & wellness holiday. But a few hours of pampering can be found on the island, for example in the independent, exclusive *Spa Líndos* (see p. 61) in the middle of the village or in the spas within some hotels. The *Lindos Blu (Tel. 22 44 03 21 10| www.lindosblu.gr)* on Vlícha Beach near Líndos is a good address and non-resident guests are welcome for the day. A popular place among locals is *Anessis Massage (daily 10am–8pm | offers from 25 euros/hr | Odós Al. Diákou 65 | tel. 22 41 02 03 02 | on Facebook)* in the New Town of Rhodes. Over 40 different massages are available. Staff will advise you on the best treatment for you which you can enjoy inside or outside under the blue skies above.

TRAVEL WITH KIDS

Rhodian children are allowed to take part in daily life in a carefree manner until long after midnight. This way, they hardly need babysitters.

They quite simply accompany the adults to cafés and tavernas that all have high chairs and the usual paper table covers on which the kids can draw. there are no special children's portions; the adults just share with them. Kids can play everywhere: church walls can be football goals, cats and dogs like to be petted. There are playgrounds, but they only fill up after 6pm and don't have sandpits because, after all, there's the beach! Special children's facilities are a rare sight in general: On Rhodes, children and adults experience everything together.

RHODES TOWN

AQUARIUM ● (U B1)

The aquarium with its wide range of species offers a great day's outing for the kids (so they can see some fish that's not on the table...). The delicate proportions of the pavilion make you think of an Art Nouveau café rather than a hydrobiological institute. The cellar of the building accommodates, apart from a marine biology museum, the fish tanks which are home to fish and other sea creatures from Greek waters, for example, bream, bass, prickly scorpion fish, sea urchin and starfish. *April–Oct. daily 9am–8:30pm, March until 4:30pm | adults 5.50 euros, children 2.50 euros | Kalímnou Lérou | www.hcmr.gr*

Look at fish today, ride a donkey tomorrow, eat ostrich eggs afterwards – lots of fun activities for the little ones

BOUNCY CASTLE (122 B1)
Shopping without the children? The bouncy castle belongs to the *Aktaíon* café (see p. 41) and offers childcare facilities by professional care assistants who check in the children and write down your mobile number on a plastic wrist strap, leaving you free to go off shopping in the city. The Platía Kyprou at the heart of the city's modern shopping street is just one minute's walk from here. When you return to pick up your kids, don't be surprised if they can speak more Greek than you can: "Éla" means "Come on!" *Daily 10am–8pm | 3.50 euros/day incl. 1 juice pack | Paidikí Chará at the Café Aktaíon | Platía Eleftherías | New Town*

MONTE SMITH (U A6)
In contrast to other ancient sites in Greece, there are no guards waiting to call kids to order if they fancy chasing each other round the track of the reconstructed stadium on Monte Smith. High above the town, they can emulate the athletes of antiquity in a truly historic set-

ting. As the site is accessible at all times, you can also choose to come in the early morning or late afternoon. *Get there via Odós Voríou Ipírou | New Town | bus no. 5 from Mandráki/Néa Agorá*

PORTRAIT ARTISTS

Numerous painters sit on the route from Mandráki Harbour to the *Pylí Agíou Pávlou Gate* (123 D2) and between the *Pyli Ambouaz Gate* and the Clock Tower (122 B3). They will draw people's portraits, either true to life or as a cartoon, depending on the sitter's wishes. A real alternative to a conventional holiday snap of your child. Prices are a matter for negotiation.

RONDINI PARK ★ (119 F2) *(🗺 H5)*

The "green lung" of Rhodes Town lies between Monte Smith and the road to Líndos. A small stream flows between pines, sycamore trees and cypresses, cascading over waterfalls and forming ponds. Stag and doe, the Rhodian heraldic animals, and also wild Cretan goats are kept in an enclosure, and peacocks parade on the pathways. There are several playgrounds scattered across the park. Rondini Park is at its prettiest in spring. Above the square, on a plateau, you can see a number of tombs cut into the rock face. Visitors to Greece in the 19th century named the finest one "The Tomb of the Ptolemies"; the locals call it *koúfio vounó*, the "hollow mountain". *Freely accessible during the day | get there via Odós Stéfanou Kasoúli or by bus no. 3 from Mandráki*

LÍNDOS AND THE SOUTH

BY DONKEY TO THE ACROPOLIS
(121 F3) *(🗺 F11)*

It must be said, riding on a donkey up to the Acropolis can be tougher and more nerve-racking for an adult than the short walk up to the top. For kids, however, it will certainly be one of the high points of the entire holiday. If the little ones then decide they'd like to ride back down again – a most costly proposition – it is probably a good idea to remind them that donkeys don't stop in front of ice-cream parlours! *6 euros per trip per person, no discount for children (fixed price, as stated in a written notice at the starting point) | starting point is the donkey "terminus" on the main road through the village between the bus stop and St Mary's Church, around 80 m/262 ft from the bus stop*

THE CENTRE

AIRPORT VIEW (118 C3) *(🗺 E6)*

In a slightly elevated position over the southeast corner of the airport grounds, sit on the terrace of a very basic café and enjoy a sensational view of the aircraft arriving and departing. It is particularly interesting when the prevailing winds come from the east, since planes always land and take off against the wind. There are plenty of children's toys available: the proprietors themselves have a large family. A baby's high chair is available, too. *Daily from 8:30am | 50 m/164 ft to the right of the road from Parádisi to Sorón | Parádisi | Budget*

FALIRÁKI WATERPARK ★
(119 F3) *(🗺 H6)*

There are seven giant water slides, up to 150 m/492 ft long, plus a so-called *Lazy River* for a leisurely ride in an inflatable boat and several swimming pools and paddling pools to cool you down. Aqua gym, waterfalls, whirlpool and wave pool: At Faliráki Water Park you'll find everything you'd expect from a modern facility of this kind. Several attractions are strictly for kids, such as the pirate's ship, equipped with water cannons, standing in the centre of a 50-cm-deep pool, or the Tarzan Pool where kids can swing on ropes across water "infested" with inflatable crocodiles. *Daily 9:30am–6:30pm | adults 24 euros, children under 3 years free; 3–12 years 16 euros | opposite the Hotel Esperides Beach | Faliráki | free bus transfer from Faliráki and Rhodes Town | www.water-park.gr*

MINIATURE TRAIN

As in many other places in Greece there are also a number of miniature trains, which run on rubber wheels, called *trenáki*. Passengers big and small sit in two or three open carriages and the trains operate on fixed routes. From the central square on the promenade in Faliráki (119 F4) (*∅ H6*) they head for the bay at Kallithéa in the morning *(duration: 135 minutes, including time for a swim)*, between 5pm and midnight there are trips every hour in and around Faliráki. *Adults 5 or 7 euros, depending on the tour; children 3 euros*

INSIDER TIP RHODES OSTRICH FARM
(119 D3) (*∅ F6*)

Over 100 ostriches clearly enjoy life on the park-like Ostrich Farm with goats, lambs, monkeys, donkeys, deer, llamas, dromedaries and kangaroos for company. You don't necessarily have to tell your children that the snack bar on the farm also sells ostrich burgers *(6 euros)* – but they probably won't object to an ostrich-egg omelette *(7 euros)*. *Daily 9am–7:30pm (or until sunset) | adults 5.50, children 3 euros, pony ride: 3 euros | 800 m (875 yd) to the right of the road from the west coast to Petaloúdes*

The Faliráki Waterpark is the perfect place for young pirates to cool off

FESTIVALS & EVENTS

The most important events of the year for the islanders are Easter and the traditional saint's days in honour of the villages' patrons. Villagers attend these parish fairs with the whole family and they are a great occasion to eat, drink and even dance: in winter during the day and in the evenings in summer. The dates of these parish festivals are irrevocable. The island also plays host to many other events and festivals. It's a good idea to watch out for posters, ask in the tourist information or look online to check the dates because the non-religious events and concerts are often announced at short notice or even cancelled.

FESTIVALS & EVENTS

MARCH–MAY

Carnival Monday: ***Colourful carnival celebrations*** in Archángelos. Everywhere else, people go out into the countryside for a picnic and to fly kites.

25 March: ***Greek national holiday*** commemorates the Greek uprising against Turkish rule in 1821; laying of wreaths and parades; children often wear traditional costume.

Good Friday: 9pm ***procession*** in all towns and villages (except in Archángelos, where it doesn't start till around midnight)

Easter Saturday: Easter mass from 11pm. Shortly before midnight, all lights in the church go out, except for the "eternal" sanctuary lamp. At midnight, the priest announces the Resurrection of Christ. All members of the congregation light candles and, outside, the young people put on a firework display with firecrackers and rockets.

Sunday after Easter: traditional ***Parish Fairs of the Churches of Ágios Thomás*** during the day in Mesanagrós and Plataniá

On a Sunday at the end of April/beginning of May: ***Roads to Rhodes*** *(www.roadstorhodes.com)*, international marathon and half-marathon starting in Rhodes Town

On seven days in mid-May: ***International Festival of Horror Films*** held in the multi-cinema complex of Cine Pállas *(Odós Dimokratías 13 | www.cinepallas.gr)* in the New Town. The films are shown in original with Greek subtitles. Last weekend in May: three-day ***medieval festival*** *(www.medievalfestival.gr)* with a market and music at the Castle of Kritiniá

JULY

16/17 July: ***Parish Fair in Koskinoú*** with bags of tradition

Celebrate festivals as they come: parish fairs are written in stone while other events are more spontaneous affairs

19 July: In the evening, large ***Parish Fair*** with traditional market at the former hotels atop Profítis Ilías
25–27 July: ***Parish Fair in Kattaviá*** with folk music and dance
29 July: In the evening ***Parish Fair at the Ágios Syllas Monastery*** near Soróni with music, dance and donkey racing

AUGUST/SEPTEMBER

First half of the month: ***Ialísia***, cultural and folklore festival in Ialissós with traditional dances, concerts, art exhibitions and sporting competitions
14–23 Aug: ***Festival of the Virgin Mary*** in Kremastí with fair, dance and music
Late August/early September: ***Wine Festival in Émbonas*** with dancing groups from all over Rhodes
7/8 Sept: ***Mass pilgrimage*** to Tsambíka Monastery. The path to the top is illuminated at night.
13–15 Sept: Large ***Parish Fair*** with traditional flair in Kallithiés

OCTOBER

Ágios Loúkas: Big ***Parish Fair*** at Afántou, 17/18 Oct

NATIONAL HOLIDAYS

The moveable feasts are scheduled according to the Julian calendar.

1 Jan	New year
6 Jan	*Epiphany*
19 Feb 2018, 11 March 2019	Carnival Monday
25 March	Greek national holiday
6 April 2018, 26 April 2019	Good Friday
8/9 April 2018, 28/29 April 2019	Easter
1 May	Labour Day
27/28 May 2018, 16/17 June 2019	Whitsun
15 Aug	Assumption
28 Oct	Greek national holiday
25/26 Dec	Christmas

LINKS, BLOGS, APPS & MORE

LINKS & BLOGS

www.rhodos-info.de/eindex.htm Website with plenty of information and tips about interesting places and beaches, plus general facts about the island

www.rodosisland.gr The website of the hoteliers' association on Rhodes features detailed information on hotel facilities and services. You can search through the choices on offer, for example, according to price category

www.rhodesguide.com Information on accommodation, events and travel tips. Great photos and videos, too

www.greeka.com/dodecanese/rhodes/ Information, photos, a travel community and clear maps of Rhodes and all the other Greek islands

www.greecetravel.com/rhodes Inside tips for Rhodes – hotels, restaurants, getting around, package tours...

http://ramblingsfromrhodes.blogspot.de British writer John Manuel, who has been living on Rhodes since 2005, writes about daily life on the island and has many good tips

http://mylittlenomads.com/rhodes-with-kids Tips, lists and personal advice specifically for family holidays on Rhodes

www.cruisetimetables.com For anyone wanting to know more about the big cruise liners that come to Rhodes harbour every day: routes and technical details of all the cruise ships

http://whc.unesco.org/en/list/493/ The medieval city of Rhodes is a Unesco World Heritage Site. The official Unesco website documents the efforts of conservation and shows pictures of the city's sights

Regardless of whether you are still preparing your trip or already on Rhodes: these addresses will provide you with more information, videos and networks to make your holiday even more enjoyable

www.facebook.com/pages/Lindos-Rhodes/28083291522?v=info Líndos visitors swap news and views on various themes to do with Líndos. The notice board also features lots of photos

twitter.com/discoverrhodes On the Twitter blog of www.discover-rhodes.com you'll find regular current news features about Rhodes, both for foreign residents of the island and tourists

VIDEOS & MUSIC

vimeo.com/6157551 First part of a private holiday video made by a Dutch traveller, including images of places and sights on Rhodes. The video has subtitles in English and links to three additional parts

www.falirakitv.com Commercial site with short videos and information, focusing especially on the nightlife in Faliráki

www.radio1.gr Private radio station on Rhodes with an English-language news programme plus international and Greek music for younger audiences.

APPS

Rhodes Island Audio Guide English-language audio guide for your smart phone. The app can be used without an Internet connection and provides information on sights, beaches and the history of the island. Short texts supplement the audio recordings, and the integrated maps are a useful aid on the ground

iSlands Island-hoppers and keen day trippers can access timetables directly from their smart phones thanks to this free app. Harbour names are given in English and Greek, which makes things easier, too

Rhodes iTour Travel Guide Finds hundreds of places on the island, from attractions to beaches, restaurants and ATMs. Events section, picture gallery, social network, radio station

Greek by Nemo, for iPhone Free, personalized language-learning app which has you speak Greek in no time!

TRAVEL TIPS

ARRIVAL

There are direct charter flights from many British airports and most major cities in Western Europe. The flight time from London is around 4 hours. Passengers on scheduled flights (almost always) have to fly via Athens. Rhodes airport lies 9 miles to the south of the capital, Rhodes Town. There is a half-hourly bus service into town.

BANKS & MONEY

It is possible to exchange money and cash traveller's cheques at banks and post offices. Opening times: *Mon–Thu 8am–2pm | Fri 8am–1:30pm*. You can also withdraw cash using your credit card at ATMs.

CONSULATES & EMBASSIES

UK EMBASSY (ATHENS)

1 Ploutarchou Street | 10675 Athens - Kolonaki | tel. 21 07 27 26 00 | www.gov.uk/government/world/organisations/british-embassy-athens

U.S. EMBASSY (ATHENS)

91 Vasilisis Sophias Avenue | 10160 Athens | tel.: 21 07 21 29 51 | athens.usembassy.gov | athensamemb@state.gov

RESPONSIBLE TRAVEL

It doesn't take a lot to be environmentally friendly whilst travelling. Don't just think about your carbon footprint whilst flying to and from your holiday destination but also about how you can protect nature and culture abroad. As a tourist it is especially important to respect nature, look out for local products, cycle instead of driving, save water and much more. If you would like to find out more about eco-tourism please visit: *www.ecotourism.org*

CUSTOMS

EU citizens can import and export goods for their personal use tax-free (800 cigarettes, 110 l of beer, 90 l of wine, 10 l of spirits). Visitors from other countries must observe the following limits, except for items for personal use. Duty free are: max. 50 g perfume, 200 cigarettes, 50 cigars, 250 g tobacco, 1 l of spirits (over 22 % vol.), 2 l of spirits (under 22 % vol.), 2 l of any wine.

DRIVING

Drivers only need to hold a valid driving licence. It is advisable to carry an international green insurance card if using your own vehicle. In the event of a breakdown, you should contact the Greek Automobile Association ELPA, on Rhodes and in the rest of Greece under the following number: *Tel. 104 00.* The statutory speed limit in built-up areas is 50 km/h (30 mph) and outside towns and villages, 90 km/h (56 mph). The maximum level of alcohol in the blood is 0.5 mg/l for car drivers and 0.2 mg/l for motorcyclists.

ELECTRICITY

Rhodes has the same 220 volt as most continental European countries. You will need an adapter if you want to use a UK plug.

EMERGENCY

Police: Tel. 112; Tourist police Rhodes Town: Tel. 22 41 02 33 29 | Odós Papágou/ Odós Makaríou)

HEALTH

General Hospital *(Jenikó Nossokomío): Rhodes Town | Leof. Georgíou Papandréou | Menkávli | tel. 22 41 08 00 00.* Chemists *(farmakíon)* are officially closed on Saturdays and Sundays. Information about out-of-hours chemists is displayed in chemists' windows. It is advisable to have an EHIC (European Health Insurance Card) or some other valid medical insurance for travel abroad.

IMMIGRATION

A valid passport is required for entry into Greece (and for excursions into Turkey). All children must travel with their own passport.

INFORMATION

GREEK NATIONAL TOURISM ORGANISATION
5th floor East, Great Portland House, 4 Great Portland Street, W1W 8QJ, London Tel. +44 20 7495 9300 www.visitgreece.gr

INTERNET & WIFI

Internet connections in Greece are just as fast and modern as in the rest of Europe, but free WiFi is available more often here than in many other places around the globe. Most hotels and guesthouses as well as tavernas, bars and cáfes – even in the most isolated villages – offer free Internet access.

NEWSPAPERS

Foreign newspapers and magazines can often be bought on the day of publication all over the island.

CURRENCY CONVERTER

£	€	€	£
1	1.40	1	0.72
3	4.17	3	2.15
5	6.96	5	3.59
13	18.08	13	9.34
40	55.65	40	28.75
75	104	75	53.89
120	167	120	86
250	348	250	180
500	696	500	359

$	€	€	$
1	0.92	1	1.09
3	2.75	3	3.27
5	4.58	5	5.45
13	11.92	13	14.18
40	36.67	40	43.64
75	69	75	81.82
120	110	120	131
250	229	250	273
500	458	500	545

For current exchange rates see www.xe.com

OPENING HOURS

Shops selling everyday tourist articles are open daily from around 10am–11pm; supermarkets generally from Monday to Saturday from 8am–8pm. Many shops which are not aimed at tourist custom remain closed on Mondays and Wednesdays in the afternoons. The opening times given in this guide for museums and archaeological excavation sites are core opening times, which are sometimes extended during high season. Most restaurants are open daily during high season.

PHONE & MOBILE PHONE

The cheapest way to phone is by using one of the many card phones which you can find even in the smallest village, but there are not very many left. Telephone cards are available from kiosks and many supermarkets for 4 euros. Mobile phone coverage is good everywhere. In some areas on the island, Turkish networks are stronger than the Greek ones and log in first. If you don't want to phone via Turkey, you must search for a different roaming partner manually.

The international dialling code for Greece is 0030. To call the UK, dial 0044, for the USA 001. Then dial the ten-digit number in Greece, in the UK and the USA, the area code without the zero.

BUDGETING

Hire car	From £ 22/$ 29 a day *for a small car*
Coffee	£ 1.30–2.20/$ 1.75–2.95 *for a cup of mocha*
Donkey ride	£ 5/$ 7 *per person in Líndos*
Umbrella	£ 5–9 /$ 7–12 *for an umbrella and two loungers at the beach*
Petrol	Around £ 1.47/$ 1.95 *for 1 l premium*
Snack	£ 2.05/$ 2.70 *for gyros and pitta bread*

POST

Post offices are generally open as follows: Mon–Fri 7:30am–3pm. Main Post Office in Rhodes Town *(Platía Dimarchíou/ Mandráki)* until 8pm. Stamps are also available (plus a surcharge) from some kiosks and hotel reception desks as well as many souvenir shops.

PRICES

Public transport is relatively cheap, food, on the other hand, expensive. Young people under 18 years of age as well as students from member states of the European Union are granted free admission to state museums and archaeological sites. Senior citizens over 65 years of age from EU countries pay reduced admission charges on presentation of their ID card or passport.

PUBLIC TRANSPORT

Buses link almost all the villages around the island with Rhodes Town. The departure point for all buses is at the back of the Néa Agorá market hall. Rhodes Town is served by seven bus lines running between about 7am and 9pm. They are run by the Roda, which is also responsible for the buses to the villages along with Ktel. Up-to-date schedules can be obtained at the *Tourist Information Offices* (see p. 46) as well as at *www.ando/gr/eot.* In the summer months, a Sea Shuttle *(www.falirakisealines.com)* runs between Faliráki and Rhodes Town four times a day from Mondays to Saturdays.

TAXI

Taxis are to be found at the airport, outside the big hotels and at the taxi rank in Rhodes Town (Mandráki Harbour). You can order one by phone under *Tel. 2241064734 or Tel. 2241064712.* You can even flag down taxis in the street. Current prices under *www.ando.gr/eot.*

TIME

Greece is two hours ahead of GMT and seven hours ahead of US Eastern Time.

TIPPING

It is customary to round the total amount up by five to ten per cent and to leave the tip on the table. Amounts under 50 cents are considered an insult.

WHEN TO GO

With the exception of the rainy and stormy months between December and mid-March, any time is a good time to visit. The island's countryside is especially lush and in full bloom between March and May. Less colourful, perhaps, but still with pleasant water temperatures, October or November are also a good choice. July and August are least suitable for hikers and those interested in visiting cultural sites due to the heat.

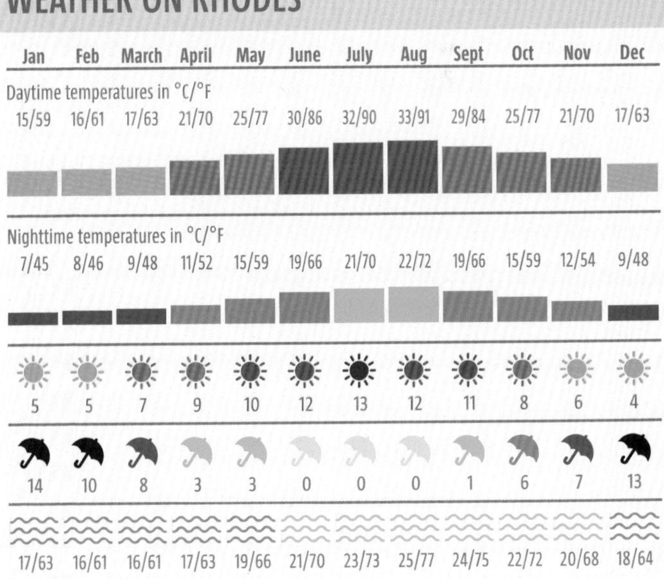

WEATHER ON RHODES

	Jan	Feb	March	April	May	June	July	Aug	Sept	Oct	Nov	Dec
Daytime temperatures in °C/°F	15/59	16/61	17/63	21/70	25/77	30/86	32/90	33/91	29/84	25/77	21/70	17/63
Nighttime temperatures in °C/°F	7/45	8/46	9/48	11/52	15/59	19/66	21/70	22/72	19/66	15/59	12/54	9/48
Sunshine hours/day	5	5	7	9	10	12	13	12	11	8	6	4
Precipitation days/month	14	10	8	3	3	0	0	0	1	6	7	13
Water temperature in °C/°F	17/63	16/61	16/61	17/63	19/66	21/70	23/73	25/77	24/75	22/72	20/68	18/64

Sunshine hours/day Precipitation days/month Water temperature in °C/°F

USEFUL PHRASES GREEK

PRONUNCIATION

We have provided a simple pronunciation aid for the Greek words (see middle column). Note the following:

' the following syllable is emphasised
ð in Greek (shown as "dh" in middle column) is like "th" in "there"
θ in Greek (shown as "th" in middle column) is like "th" in "think"
X in Greek (shown as "ch" in middle column) is like a rough "h" or "ch" in Scottish "loch"

Α	α	a	Η	η	i	Ν	ν	n	Τ	τ	t
Β	β	v	Θ	θ	th	Ξ	ξ	ks, x	Υ	υ	i, y
Γ	γ	g, y	Ι	ι	i, y	Ο	ο	o	Φ	φ	f
Δ	δ	th	Κ	κ	k	Π	π	p	Χ	χ	ch
Ε	ε	e	Λ	λ	l	Ρ	ρ	r	Ψ	ψ	ps
Ζ	ζ	z	Μ	μ	m	Σ	σ, ς	s, ss	Ω	ώ	o

IN BRIEF

Yes/No/Maybe	ne/'ochi/'issos	Ναι/ Όχι/Ισως
Please/Thank you	paraka'lo/efcharis'to	Παρακαλώ/Ευχαριστώ
Sorry	sig'nomi	Συγνώμη
Excuse me	me sig'chorite	Με συγχωρείτε
May I...?	epi'treppete...?	Επιτρέπεται…?
Pardon?	o'riste?	Ορίστε?
I would like to.../	'thelo.../	Θέλω…/
have you got...?	'echete...?	Έχετε…?
How much is...?	'posso 'kani...?	Πόσο κάνει…?
I (don't) like this	Af'to (dhen) mu a'ressi	Αυτό (δεν) μου αρέσει
good/bad	ka'llo/kak'ko	καλό/κακό
too much/much/little	'para pol'li/pol'li/'ligo	πάρα πολύ/πολύ/λίγο
everything/nothing	ólla/'tipottal	όλα/τίποτα
Help!/Attention!/	vo'ithia!/prosso'chi!/	Βοήθεια!/Προσοχή!/
Caution!	prosso'chi!	Προσοχή!
ambulance	astheno'forro	Ασθενοφόρο
police/	astino'mia/	Αστυνομία/
fire brigade	pirosvesti'ki	Πυροσβεστική
ban/	apa'gorefsi/	Απαγόρευση/
forbidden	apago'revete	απαγορεύεται
danger/dangerous	'kindinoss/epi'kindinoss	Κίνδυνος/επικίνδυνος

Milás elliniká?

"Do you speak Greek?" This guide will help you to say the basic words and phrases in Greek.

GREETINGS, FAREWELL

Good morning!/after-noon!/evening!/night!	kalli'mera/kalli'mera!/ kalli'spera!/kalli'nichta!	Καλημέρα/Καλημέρα!/ Καλησπέρα!/Καληνύχτα!
Hello!/ goodbye!	'ya (su/sass)!/a'dio!/ ya (su/sass)!	Γεία (σου/σας)!/αντίο!/ Γεία (σου/σας)!
Bye!	me 'lene...	Με λένε…
My name is...	poss sass 'lene?	Πως σας λένε?

DATE & TIME

Monday/Tuesday	dhef'tera/'triti	Δευτέρα/Τρίτη
Wednesday/Thursday	tet'tarti/'pempti	Τετάρτη/Πέμπτη
Friday/Saturday	paraske'vi/'savatto	Παρασκευή/Σάββατο
Sunday/weekday	kiria'ki/er'gassimi	Κυριακή/Εργάσιμη
today/tomorrow/yesterday	'simera/'avrio/chtess	Σήμερα/Αύριο/Χτες
What time is it?	ti 'ora 'ine?	Τι ώρα είναι?

TRAVEL

open/closed	annik'ta/klis'to	Ανοικτό/Κλειστό
entrance/ driveway	'issodhos/ 'issodhos ochi'matonn	Έισοδος/ Έισοδος οχημάτων
exit/exit	'eksodhos/ 'Eksodos ochi'matonn	Έξοδος/ Έξοδος οχημάτων
departure/ departure/arrival	anna'chorissi/ anna'chorissi/'afiksi	Αναχώρηση/ Αναχώρηση/Άφιξη
toilets/restrooms / ladies/ gentlemen	tual'lettes/gine'konn/ an'dronn	Τουαλέτες/Γυναικών/ Ανδρών
(no) drinking water	'possimo ne'ro	Πόσιμο νερό
Where is...?/Where are...?	pu 'ine...?/pu 'ine...?	Πού είναι/Πού είναι…?
bus/taxi	leofo'rio/tak'si	Λεωφορείο/Ταξί
street map/ map	'chartis tis 'pollis/ 'chartis	Χάρτης της πόλης/ Χάρτης
harbour	li'mani	Λιμάνι
airport	a-ero'drommio	Αεροδρόμιο
schedule/ticket	drommo'logio/issi'tirio	Δρομολόγιο/Εισιτήριο
I would like to rent...	'thelo na nik'yasso...	Θέλω να νοικιάσω…
a car/a bicycle/ a boat	'enna afto'kinito/'enna po'dhilato/'mia 'varka	ένα αυτοκίνητο/ένα ποδήλατο/μία βάρκα
petrol/gas station	venzi'nadiko	Βενζινάδικο
petrol/gas / diesel	ven'zini/'diesel	Βενζίνη/Ντίζελ

FOOD & DRINK

Could you please book a table for tonight for four?	Klis'te mass parakal'lo 'enna tra'pezi ya a'popse ya 'tessera 'atoma	Κλείστε μας παρακαλώ ένα τραπέζι γιά απόψε γιά τέσσερα άτομα
The menu, please	tonn ka'taloggo parakal'lo	Τον κατάλογο παρακαλώ
Could I please have...?	tha 'ithella na 'echo...?	Θα ήθελα να έχο…?
with/without ice/ sparkling	me/cho'ris 'pago/ anthrakik'ko	με/χωρίς πάγο/ ανθρακικό
vegetarian/allergy	chorto'fagos/allerg'ia	Χορτοφάγος/Αλλεργία
May I have the bill, please?	'thel'lo na pli'rosso parakal'lo	Θέλω να πληρώσω παρακαλώ

SHOPPING

Where can I find...?	pu tha vro...?	Που θα βρω…?
pharmacy/ chemist	farma'kio/ ka'tastima	Φαρμακείο/Κατάστημα καλλυντικών
bakery/market	'furnos/ago'ra	Φούρνος/Αγορά
grocery	pandopo'lio	Παντοπωλείο
kiosk	pe'riptero	Περίπτερο
expensive/cheap/price	akri'vos/fti'nos/ti'mi	ακριβός/φτηνός/Τιμή
more/less	pio/li'gotere	πιό/λιγότερο

ACCOMMODATION

I have booked a room	'kratissa 'enna do'matio	Κράτησα ένα δωμάτιο
Do you have any... left?	'echete a'komma...	Έχετε ακόμα…
single room	mon'noklino	Μονόκλινο
double room	'diklino	Δίκλινο
key	kli'dhi	Κλειδί
room card	ilektronni'ko kli'dhi	Ηλεκτρονικό κλειδί

HEALTH

doctor/dentist/ paediatrician	ya'tros/odhondoya'tros/ pe'dhiatros	Ιατρός/Οδοντογιατρός/ Παιδίατρος
hospital/ emergency clinic	nossoko'mio/ yatri'ko 'kentro	Νοσοκομείο/ Ιατρικό κέντρο
fever/pain	piret'tos/'ponnos	Πυρετός/Πόνος
diarrhoea/nausea	dhi'arria/ana'gula	Διάρροια/Αναγούλα
sunburn	ilia'ko 'engavma	Ηλιακό έγκαυμα
inflamed/ injured	molli'menno/ pligo'menno	μολυμένο /πληγωμένο
pain reliever/tablet	paf'siponna/'chapi	Παυσίπονο/Χάπι

POST, TELECOMMUNICATIONS & MEDIA

stamp/letter	gramma'tossimo/'gramma	Γραμματόσημο/Γράμμα
postcard	kartpos'tall	Καρτ-ποστάλ
I need a landline phone card	kri'azomme 'mia tile'karta ya dhi'mossio tilefoni'ko 'thalamo	Χρειάζομαι μία τηλεκάρτα για δημόσιο τηλεφωνικό θάλαμο
I'm looking for a prepaid card for my mobile	tha 'ithella 'mia 'karta ya to kinni'to mu	Θα ήθελα μία κάρτα για το κινητό μου
Where can I find internet access?	pu bor'ro na vro 'prosvassi sto índernett?	Που μπορώ να βρω πρόσβαση στο ίντερνετ?
socket/adapter/ charger	'briza/an'dapporras/ fortis'tis	πρίζα/αντάπτορας/ φορτιστής
computer/battery/ rechargeable battery	ippologis'tis/batta'ria/ eppanaforti'zomenni batta'ria	Υπολογιστής/μπαταρία/ επαναφορτιζόμενη μπαταρία
internet connection/ wifi	'sindhessi se as'sirmato 'dhitio/vaifai	Σύνδεση σε ασύρματο δίκτυο/WiFi

LEISURE, SPORTS & BEACH

beach	para'lia	Παραλία
sunshade/lounger	om'brella/ksap'plostra	Ομπρέλα/Ξαπλώστρα

NUMBERS

0	mi'dhen	μηδέν
1	'enna	ένα
2	'dhio	δύο
3	'tria	τρία
4	'tessera	τέσσερα
5	'pende	πέντε
6	'eksi	έξι
7	ef'ta	εφτά
8	och'to	οχτώ
9	e'nea	εννέα
10	'dhekka	δέκα
11	'endhekka	ένδεκα
12	'dodhekka	δώδεκα
20	'ikossi	είκοσι
50	pen'inda	πενήντα
100	eka'to	εκατό
200	dhia'kossia	διακόσια
1000	'chilia	χίλια
10000	'dhekka chil'iades	δέκα χιλιάδες

ROAD ATLAS

The green line indicates the Discovery Tour "Rhodes at a glance"
The blue line indicates the other Discovery Tours

All tours are also marked on the pull-out map

 Photo: Lindos

Exploring Rhodes

The map on the back cover shows how the area has been sub-divided

A
B
C
1
2
3
4
5
6
Alimiá
Αλιμιά
Vouní
268
Alimiá
Katsoúni
Ágios Theodóros
Ormos Alimias
Ág. Minas
Akra Mermingas
126
Hálki
Χάλκη
Akra Kefálos
Akra Armeno
Akra Limanari
Maistros
593
Emborió
Εμπορειό
Profítis Ilías
483
Ág. Marina
441
Moní Ág. Ioánnis
Horió
288
Pontamos
Krevati
Nisaki
Tragoussa
Akra Mírtos
Akra Íkalos
Diafáni (Kárpathos)
M E D I T E R R A N E A N
S E A
P. Soroní
P. Fanou
P. Anomomilos
Gefira Fanou
16
Akra Minas
Fánes
Kalavárda
198
13
Kamiros
★★
Ág. Faneroméni
Argiros
Plati
16
277
Chalki
1
27
Mandrikó
(210)
Salakos
Σάλακος
Dimiliá
Akra Kopriá
Kapí
15
Élafos-Elafiná
Kástellos Kritinia
Skala Kamiros
Nani
3
714
Athlitikó Kentro
798
Profítis Ilías
Platáni
Mousio
Moní Karlóna
(310)
Apóllona
Απόλλωνα
Kritinía
Κρητηνία
504
12
301
Moní Amartos
Amartos
Emery
Émbonas
Έμπωνας
342
Atáviros
1216
367
Assouri
403
Moní Artamiti
360
Stavrós
Atáviros
1071
120

D
E
F
1
2
3
4
5
6
Ródos
Kamiros
Skala Kamiros
Akra Kopriá
Kástellos
Kritinía
Makri
Strongili
P. Paleóhora
Moní Amartos
Amartos
342
Ormos
Glifádas
Lakkí
Sími
Kós
Pireás
Marmaris
Fethiye
Bodrum
Megísti
Lemesós
Akra Zonári
Enidríou
RÓDOS
ΡΌΔΟΣ
Paláti Ippotón
Monte Smith
KRÍTIKA
KANDILION
Emborió (Hálki)
IALISÓS (TRIÁNTA)
ΙΑΛΥΣΌΣ (ΤΡΙΆΝΤΑ)
Kremastí
Κρεμαστή
P. Ialisso
Ormos Triánta
IXIA
P. Ixia
Gefira Kremastí
Diagoras International Airport
RHO
Panagía Kremastí
Ág. Ioánnis
TREIS
Rodini Parko
Ág. Marina
Sgouroú (Asgourou)
Kallithea
Akra Vódi
EO95
Paradisi
Παραδείσι
Paradísi Airstrip
267
Filérimos
Ialisos
Pastida
Παστίδα
Thoíos
Káto Kalamónas
Theológos
Damatría
EO95a
Koskinoú
Κοσκινού
Thermes Kallithéas
Ormos Kallithéas
P. Faliráki
Maritsá
Μαριτσά
263
418
Koumoúlia
Epanó Kalamónas
Rodos Ostrich Farm
Moní Ágios Eleoúsas
Ágios Ioánnis
Kalithiés
Καλνθιές
Faliráki
Petaloúdes
Moní Kalópetras
Moní Profitis Amos
Anthony Quinn Bay
Akra Ladikoú
P. Ladikoú
Psínthos
Ψίνθος
Ág. Geórgios
330
Psalídi
485
Psínthos
382
Alogna
P. Traganoú
Ág. Triada
Afándou
ΑΦάντου
P. Afándou
Katholikí Afándou
411
Ormos Afándou
Panagía Parmenitissis
Eleoússa
Moní Panagía Paramithias
Gefira Loutáni
Kolímbia
Loutan
Arhípoli
Αρχίπολη
Ág. Nektários
465
Ág. Thomas
Akra Vágia
551
Eptá Pigés
341
Messovouna
Panagía Tsambíka
Moní Tsambíka
Paralia Tsambíkas
Platanero
Ormos Arhángelou
Petrona
P. Stegná
Stegná
Arhángelos
Αρχάγγελος
Makkaris
Malónas
Μαλώνας
512
Profitis Ílias
4 km
2.5 mi
324
Akra Arhángelos
Moní Kamírou
Ormos Malónos
119
121
Másari
P. Ag. Agathi
Kastro Feráklos
218

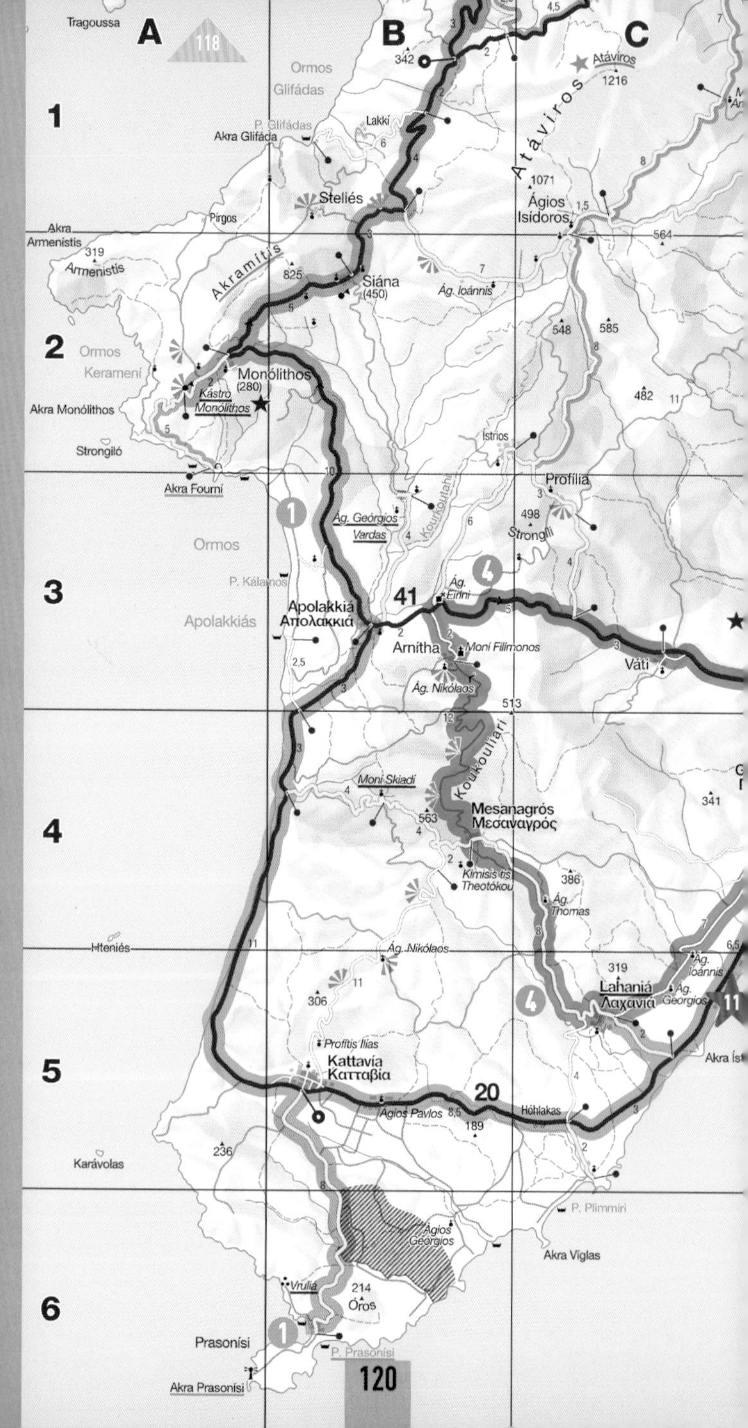

A
B
C
118
1
2
3
4
5
6
Tragoussa
Ormos
Glifádas
P. Glifádas
Akra Glifáda
Lakkí
Steliés
Pirgos
Akra Armenistis
319
Armenistis
Akramítis
825
Siána
(450)
Ág. Ioánnis
Atáviros
1216
Atáviros
1071
Ágios Isídoros
564
342
548
585
482
Ormos Kerameni
Monólithos
(280)
Kástro Monólithos
Akra Monólithos
Strongiló
Akra Fourní
Ístrios
Profília
498
Strongíli
Ág. Geórgios Vardas
Koukoutahi
Ormos
Apolakkiás
P. Kálamos
Apolakkiá
Απολακκιά
41
Ág. Eiríni
Arnítha
Moní Filímonos
Ág. Nikólaos
Váti
513
Koukouliari
Moní Skiadí
563
Mesanagrós
Μεσαναγρός
341
Kímisis tis Theotókou
386
Ág. Thomas
Hteniés
Ág. Nikólaos
306
319
Lahaniá
Λαχανιά
Ág. Ioánnis
Ág. Georgios
Akra Íst
Profítis Ílias
Kattavía
Καττάβια
20
Ágios Pavlos
189
Hóhlakas
236
Karávolas
P. Plimmíri
Ágios Georgios
Akra Víglas
Vruliá
214
Óros
Prasonísi
P. Prasonísi
Akra Prasonísi

D
E
F
Arhángelos
Αρχάγγελος
Malónas
Μαλώνας
Petrona
Profitis Ílias
Ormos Malónos
P. Ag. Agathí
Kastro Feráklos
Haráki
P. Másari
Másari
Moní Kamírou
Ág. Geórgios Lorima
Gaidourás
Gefira Gaidourás
Ormos Renis
Assoun
Stavrós
Láerma
Λάερμα
Moní Thári
Kálathos
Κάλαθος
Ormos Vlihá
P. Vlihá
Vlihá
EO95
Akra Ág. Emilianós
Inko
Moní Inko
Moní Ipsenís
Pilónas
Lárdos
Λάρδος
Marmári
Líndos
Λίνδος
Ormos Líndou
Akropolí lís Líndou
Lim. Apostolou Pavlou
Ág. Geórgios
Kontar
Asklipiío
Pendánisi
P. Lárdos
P. Lothiarka
Péfki
P. Glístra
Ormos Lárdou
Pénde Vráhi
Akra Lárdos
Kiotári
P. Kiotári
Ormos Gennádiou
P. Gennadi
Lahaniá
MEDITERRANEAN SEA
4 km
2.5 mi

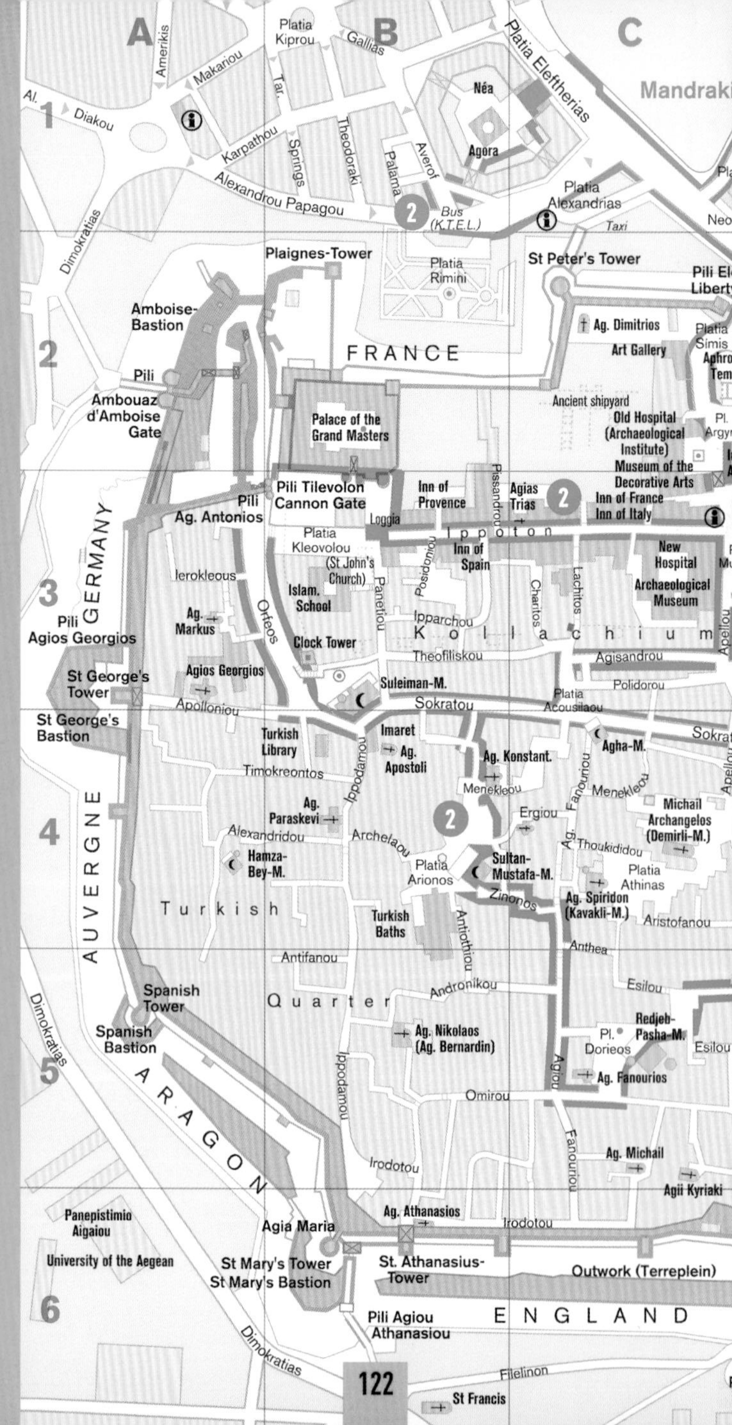

A
B
C
1
2
3
4
5
6
Mandraki
Amerikis
Platia Kiprou
Gallias
Makariou
Al. Diakou
Tar.
Karpathou
Springs
Theodoraki
Palama
Averof
Néa Agora
Platia Eleftherias
Alexandrou Papagou
Bus (K.T.E.L.)
Platia Alexandrias
Taxi
Dimokratias
Plaignes-Tower
Platia Rimini
St Peter's Tower
Pili Eleftherias Liberty
Ag. Dimitrios
Art Gallery
Platia Simis
Amboise-Bastion
FRANCE
Pili
Ambouaz d'Amboise Gate
Ancient shipyard
Old Hospital (Archaeological Institute)
Palace of the Grand Masters
Museum of the Decorative Arts
Pili Tilevolon Cannon Gate
Inn of Provence
Pissandrou
Agias Trias
Inn of France
Inn of Italy
Pili Ag. Antonios
Loggia
Ippoton
GERMANY
Platia Kleovolou
(St John's Church)
Inn of Spain
New Hospital
Archaeological Museum
Ierokleous
Islam. School
Paneriou
Posidoniou
Charitos
Lachitos
Pili Agios Georgios
Ag. Markus
Orfeos
Ipparchou
Kollachium
Apellou
Clock Tower
Theofiliskou
Agisandrou
Agios Georgios
St George's Tower
Suleiman-M.
Polidorou
Apolloniou
Sokratou
Platia Acousilaou
St George's Bastion
Turkish Library
Imaret
Ag. Apostoli
Ag. Konstant.
Agha-M.
Timokreontos
Ippodamou
Menekleou
Fanouriou
Ag. Paraskevi
Ergiou
Michail Archangelos (Demirli-M.)
AUVERGNE
Alexandridou
Archelaou
Thoukididou
Hamza-Bey-M.
Platia Arionos
Sultan-Mustafa-M.
Platia Athinas
Zinonos
Ag. Spiridon (Kavakli-M.)
Turkish
Turkish Baths
Antiothiou
Aristofanou
Antifanou
Anthea
Andronikou
Esilou
Spanish Tower
Quarter
Dimokratias
Spanish Bastion
Ag. Nikolaos (Ag. Bernardin)
Redjeb-Pasha-M.
Pl. Dorieos
Agiou
ARAGON
Ag. Fanourios
Omirou
Ag. Michail
Irodotou
Agii Kyriaki
Panepistimio Aigaiou
Ag. Athanasios
Irodotou
Agia Maria
University of the Aegean
St Mary's Tower
St Mary's Bastion
St. Athanasius-Tower
Outwork (Terreplein)
ENGLAND
Pili Agiou Athanasiou
Dimokratias
Filelinon
St Francis

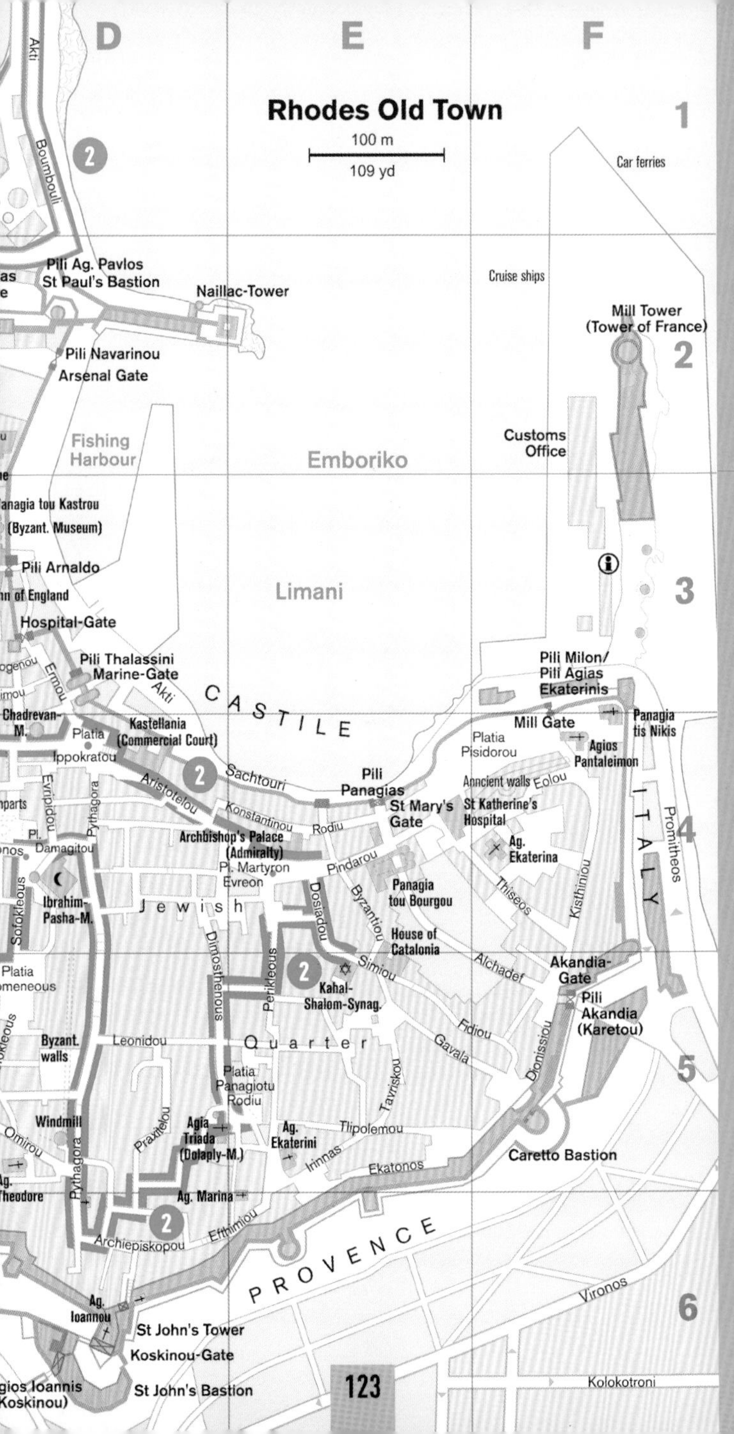

Rhodes Old Town
100 m
109 yd
D
E
F
1
2
3
4
5
6
Car ferries
Cruise ships
Pili Ag. Pavlos
St Paul's Bastion
Naillac-Tower
Mill Tower
(Tower of France)
Pili Navarinou
Arsenal Gate
Fishing
Harbour
Emboriko
Customs
Office
Panagia tou Kastrou
(Byzant. Museum)
Pili Arnaldo
Limani
Hospital-Gate
Pili Thalassini
Marine-Gate
Pili Milon/
Pili Agias
Ekaterinis
CASTILE
Chadrevan-
M.
Kastellania
(Commercial Court)
Mill Gate
Panagia
tis Nikis
Agios
Pantaleimon
Platia
Pisidorou
Ippokratou
Sachtouri
Pili
Panagias
St Mary's
Gate
Anncient walls
Eolou
St Katherine's
Hospital
Aristotelou
Konstantinou
Rodiu
Archbishop's Palace
(Admiralty)
Ag.
Ekaterina
Pl. Martyron
Evreon
Pindarou
Damagitou
Ibrahim-
Pasha-M.
Jewish
Quarter
Panagia
tou Bourgou
Thiseos
Kisthiniou
ITALY
Promitheos
House of
Catalonia
Dosiadou
Byzantiou
Simiou
Alchadef
Akandia-
Gate
Pili
Akandia
(Karetou)
Kahal-
Shalom-Synag.
Dimosthenous
Perikleous
Fidiou
Gavala
Dionissiou
Byzant.
walls
Leonidou
Platia
Panagiotu
Rodiu
Tavriskou
Windmill
Omirou
Agia
Triada
(Dolaply-M.)
Ag.
Ekaterini
Tlipolemou
Irinnas
Caretto Bastion
Ekatonos
Ag.
Theodore
Ag. Marina
Pythagora
Praxitelou
Archiepiskopou
Efthimiou
PROVENCE
Vironos
Ag.
Ioannou
St John's Tower
Koskinou-Gate
Agios Ioannis
(Koskinou)
St John's Bastion
Kolokotroni
Akti
Boumbouli
Ermou
Evripidou
Sofokleous

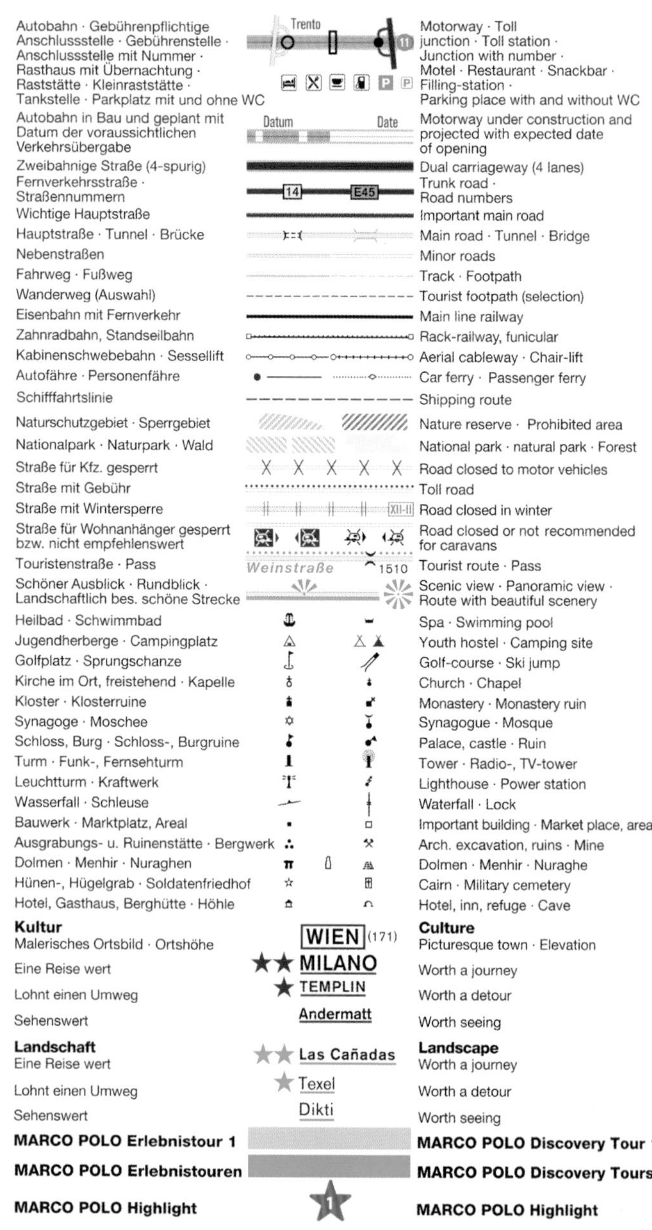
Autobahn · Gebührenpflichtige Anschlussstelle · Gebührenstelle · Anschlussstelle mit Nummer · Rasthaus mit Übernachtung · Raststätte · Kleinraststätte · Tankstelle · Parkplatz mit und ohne WC
Trento
11
P
Motorway · Toll junction · Toll station · Junction with number · Motel · Restaurant · Snackbar · Filling-station · Parking place with and without WC
Autobahn in Bau und geplant mit Datum der voraussichtlichen Verkehrsübergabe
Datum
Date
Motorway under construction and projected with expected date of opening
Zweibahnige Straße (4-spurig)
Dual carriageway (4 lanes)
Fernverkehrsstraße · Straßennummern
14
E45
Trunk road · Road numbers
Wichtige Hauptstraße
Important main road
Hauptstraße · Tunnel · Brücke
Main road · Tunnel · Bridge
Nebenstraßen
Minor roads
Fahrweg · Fußweg
Track · Footpath
Wanderweg (Auswahl)
Tourist footpath (selection)
Eisenbahn mit Fernverkehr
Main line railway
Zahnradbahn, Standseilbahn
Rack-railway, funicular
Kabinenschwebebahn · Sessellift
Aerial cableway · Chair-lift
Autofähre · Personenfähre
Car ferry · Passenger ferry
Schifffahrtslinie
Shipping route
Naturschutzgebiet · Sperrgebiet
Nature reserve · Prohibited area
Nationalpark · Naturpark · Wald
National park · natural park · Forest
Straße für Kfz. gesperrt
Road closed to motor vehicles
Straße mit Gebühr
Toll road
Straße mit Wintersperre
XII-II
Road closed in winter
Straße für Wohnanhänger gesperrt bzw. nicht empfehlenswert
Road closed or not recommended for caravans
Touristenstraße · Pass
Weinstraße
1510
Tourist route · Pass
Schöner Ausblick · Rundblick · Landschaftlich bes. schöne Strecke
Scenic view · Panoramic view · Route with beautiful scenery
Heilbad · Schwimmbad
Spa · Swimming pool
Jugendherberge · Campingplatz
Youth hostel · Camping site
Golfplatz · Sprungschanze
Golf-course · Ski jump
Kirche im Ort, freistehend · Kapelle
Church · Chapel
Kloster · Klosterruine
Monastery · Monastery ruin
Synagoge · Moschee
Synagogue · Mosque
Schloss, Burg · Schloss-, Burgruine
Palace, castle · Ruin
Turm · Funk-, Fernsehturm
Tower · Radio-, TV-tower
Leuchtturm · Kraftwerk
Lighthouse · Power station
Wasserfall · Schleuse
Waterfall · Lock
Bauwerk · Marktplatz, Areal
Important building · Market place, area
Ausgrabungs- u. Ruinenstätte · Bergwerk
Arch. excavation, ruins · Mine
Dolmen · Menhir · Nuraghen
Dolmen · Menhir · Nuraghe
Hünen-, Hügelgrab · Soldatenfriedhof
Cairn · Military cemetery
Hotel, Gasthaus, Berghütte · Höhle
Hotel, inn, refuge · Cave
Kultur
Culture
Malerisches Ortsbild · Ortshöhe
WIEN (171)
Picturesque town · Elevation
Eine Reise wert
MILANO
Worth a journey
Lohnt einen Umweg
TEMPLIN
Worth a detour
Sehenswert
Andermatt
Worth seeing
Landschaft
Landscape
Eine Reise wert
Las Cañadas
Worth a journey
Lohnt einen Umweg
Texel
Worth a detour
Sehenswert
Dikti
Worth seeing
MARCO POLO Erlebnistour 1
MARCO POLO Discovery Tour 1
MARCO POLO Erlebnistouren
MARCO POLO Discovery Tours
MARCO POLO Highlight
1
MARCO POLO Highlight

MARCO POLO TRAVEL GUIDES

Algarve
Amsterdam
Andalucia
Athens
Australia
Austria
Bali & Lombok
Bangkok
Barcelona
Berlin
Brazil
Bruges
Brussels
Budapest
Bulgaria
California
Cambodia
Canada East
Canada West / Rockies & Vancouver
Cape Town & Garden Route
Cape Verde
Channel Islands
Chicago & The Lakes
China
Cologne
Copenhagen
Corfu
Costa Blanca & Valencia
Costa Brava
Costa del Sol & Granada
Crete
Cuba
Cyprus (North and South)
Devon & Cornwall
Dresden
Dubai
Dublin
Dubrovnik & Dalmatian Coast
Edinburgh
Egypt
Egypt Red Sea Resorts
Finland
Florence
Florida
French Atlantic Coast
French Riviera (Nice, Cannes & Monaco)
Fuerteventura
Gran Canaria
Greece
Hamburg
Hong Kong & Macau
Iceland
India
India South
Ireland
Israel
Istanbul
Italy
Japan
Jordan
Kos
Krakow
Lake Garda
Lanzarote
Las Vegas
Lisbon
London
Los Angeles
Madeira & Porto Santo
Madrid
Mallorca
Malta & Gozo
Mauritius
Menorca
Milan
Montenegro
Morocco
Munich
Naples & Amalfi Coast
New York
New Zealand
Norway
Oslo
Oxford
Paris
Peru & Bolivia
Phuket
Portugal
Prague
Rhodes
Rome
Salzburg
San Francisco
Santorini
Sardinia
Scotland
Seychelles
Shanghai
Sicily
Singapore
South Africa
Sri Lanka
Stockholm
Switzerland
Tenerife
Thailand
Turkey
Turkey South Coast
Tuscany
United Arab Emirates
USA Southwest (Las Vegas, Colorado, New Mexico, Arizona & Utah)
Venice
Vienna
Vietnam
Zakynthos & Ithaca, Kefalonia, Lefkas

INDEX

This index lists all main places and popular destinations featured in this guide, as well as important terms and personal names. Numbers in bold indicate a main entry.

WRITE TO US

e-mail: info@marcopologuides.co.uk

Did you have a great holiday?
Is there something on your mind?
Whatever it is, let us know!
Whether you want to praise, alert us to errors or give us a personal tip – MARCO POLO would be pleased to hear from you.
We do everything we can to provide the very latest information for your trip. Nevertheless, despite all of our authors' thorough research, errors can creep in. MARCO POLO does not accept any liability for this. Please contact us by e-mail or post.

MARCO POLO Travel Publishing Ltd
Pinewood, Chineham Business Park
Crockford Lane, Chineham
Basingstoke, Hampshire RG24 8AL
United Kingdom

PICTURE CREDITS
Cover photograph: Mandráki Harbour (Schapowalow/SIME: L. Da Ros)
Photos: W. Dieterich (flap left, 4 top, 7, 12/13, 17, 30, 43, 47, 50/51, 68/69, 79, 84/85); F. M. Frei (90, 106 top); Getty Images: P. Fenn (104), J. Greuel (24/25), Maremagnum (38/39); Getty Images/EyesWideOpen (flap right); Getty Images/StockFood (104/105); Getty Images/Westend61 (3); R. Hackenberg (8, 14/15, 80/81); huber-images: L. Da Ros (37, 54/55, 99), D. Erbetta (75), Kaos03 (26/27), M. Ripani (2), Schmid (28 left); © iStockphoto: Robert Kohlhuber (19 top); S. Kuttig (31, 57); Laif: J. Gläscher (100/101), B. Jaschinski (20/21), F. Tophoven (9); Laif/hemis.fr: R. Soberka (44); Laif/robertharding: N. Farrin (6); H. Leue (107); Look: I. Pompe (4 bottom, 59, 61, 76), H. Wohner (58, 116/117); Look/age fotostock (72, 106 bottom); mauritius images: S. Beuthan (41), R. Hackenberg (18 bottom, 70), Maskot (19 bottom), Merten (11); mauritius images/age (63); mauritius images/Alamy: G. B. Evans (103), Lagoon Images (29), R. Savran (18 top); mauritius images/Caia Image: T. Adeline (96/97); mauritius images/Food and Drink (28 right); mauritius images/imagebroker: Ch. Handl (66, 94/95), T. Haupt (82/83), M. Nitzschke (10); mauritius images/Radius Images (52); mauritius images/robertharding: R. Tomlinson (48/49); mauritius images/TPP: Y. Shal (5, 18 centre); mauritius images/Westend61: T. Haupt (32/33); picture-alliance/akg-images (22); Schapowalow/SIME: L. Da Ros (1), J. Huber (64/65); E. Wrba (30/31, 34, 36, 105)

3rd Edition – fully revised and updated 2018
Worldwide Distribution: Marco Polo Travel Publishing Ltd, Pinewood, Chineham Business Park, Crockford Lane, Basingstoke, Hampshire RG24 8AL, United Kingdom. Email: sales@marcopolouk.com

Chief editor: Marion Zorn
Author: Klaus Bötig; Editor: Franziska Kahl
Programme supervision: Lucas Forst-Gill, Susanne Heimburger, Johanna Jiranek, Nikolai Michaelis, Kristin Wittemann, Tim Wohlbold
Picture editors: Gabriele Forst, Anja Schlatterer; What's hot: wunder media, Munich; Cartography road atlas and pull-out map: © MAIRDUMONT, Ostfildern; Design cover, p. 1, cover pull-out map: Karl Anders – Büro für Visual Stories, Hamburg; interior design: milchhof:atelier, Berlin; p. 2/ 3, Discovery Tours: Susan Chaaban Dipl.-Des. (FH)
Translated from German by Susan Jones, Jane Riester, Jennifer Walcoff Neuheiser; Prepress: writehouse, Cologne; InterMedia, Ratingen
Phrase book in cooperation with Ernst Klett Sprachen GmbH, Stuttgart, Editorial by Pons Wörterbücher

Printed in China

DOS & DON'TS 

Things to avoid to make sure your Rhodes holiday is a real success

LET YOURSELF BE INTIMIDATED

Tour guides live partly off their commission, and the big tour operators factor them in from the beginning. Almost all tour guides are honest and inform their guests truthfully about their holiday destination. Some black sheep, however, try to generate a degree of anxiety in their clients to make sure they book their hire cars through them and only take part in organised excursions instead of travelling by bus or taxi. Rhodes is in all respects a safe island, and there is no need to be wary of the local residents. Late at night in the centre of Faliráki, perhaps, you should be wary of mostly young British hooligans who unfortunately much too often start a drunken brawl.

SHOOT TO KILL (WITH YOUR CAMERA)

Many Rhodians enjoy being photographed but hate it when tourists behave like hunters who shoot anything that moves! Before you press the shutter release on your camera, be sure to get permission from your live "motif" with a smile first.

DRESS TOO SCANTILY

At the beach and in the tourist resorts Greeks have got used to the sight of plenty of bare skin. In the villages of the interior and in the Old Town, however, scanty clothing is inappropriate. In churches and monasteries, knees and shoulders must be covered, though it is not necessary for women to wear a headscarf.

BE SURPRISED AT THE PRICE OF FISH

Fresh fish is absurdly expensive in restaurants and tavernas in Greece. You should always ask the price per kilo and watch the fish being weighed in order to avoid unpleasant surprises when presented with the bill.

UNDERESTIMATE THE DANGER OF FIRE

The risk of forest fires in Rhodes is high. Smokers are therefore asked to be particularly careful.

FORGET TO BEEP

Greeks are masters of the art of cutting corners. Keep to the right on the road and sound your horn on blind corners.

SUCCUMB TO THE KIR ROYAL

Jewellers and fur dealers like to treat visitors to their shops to a glass of kir royal, whisky, ouzo or sparkling wine while making their sales pitch. Maybe they think their clients can be more easily cajoled into making a purchase this way.

MAKE DOWN PAYMENTS

Rhodian hoteliers and holiday apartment owners often demand high down payments or even payment in advance from customers who book directly. If you are unfamiliar with the accommodation you should at most agree to a credit card guarantee for the first night.